LIBRARY TRAINING GUIDES

Series Editor: David Baker
Editorial Assistant: Joan Welsby

Other Library Training Guides available

Training needs analysis
Michael Williamson
1-85604-077-1

Induction
Julie Parry
1-85604-078-X

Evaluation
Steve Phillips
1-85604-079-8

Training and development for women
Beryl Morris
1-85604-080-1

Interpersonal skills
Philippa Levy
1-85604-081-X

Management of training and staff development
June Whetherly
1-85604-104-2

Mentoring
Biddy Fisher
1-85604-105-0

Recruitment
Julie Parry
1-85604-106-9

Supporting adult learners
Tony Bamber *et al.*
1-85604-125-5

Presenting information
Clare Nankivell and Michael Shoolbred
1-85604-138-7

Personal professional development and the solo librarian
Sue Lacey Bryant
1-85604-141-7

Team management
Robert Bluck
1-85604-167-0

Training library assistants
Margaret Lobban
1-85604-139-5

Training for IT
Richard Biddiscombe
1-85604-186-7

Introduction by the Series Editor

This series of Library Training Guides (LTGs for short) aims to fill the gap left by the demise of the old Training Guidelines published in the 1980s in the wake of The Library Association's work on staff training. The LTGs develop the original concept of concisely written summaries of the best principles and practice in specific areas of training by experts in the field which give library and information workers a good-quality guide to best practice. Like the original guidelines, the LTGs also include appropriate examples from a variety of library systems as well as further reading and useful contacts.

Though each guide stands in its own right, LTGs form a coherent whole. Acquisition of all LTGs as they are published will result in a comprehensive manual of training and staff development in library and information work.

The guides are aimed at practising librarians and library training officers. They are intended to be comprehensive without being over-detailed; they should give both the novice and the experienced librarian/training officer an overview of what should/could be done in a given situation and in relation to a particular skill/group of library staff/type of library.

David Baker

LIBRARY TRAINING GUIDES

Achieving Change Through Training and Development

June Whetherly

Library Association Publishing

© The Library Association 1998

Published by
Library Association Publishing
7 Ridgmount Street
London WC1E 7AE

Library Association Publishing is wholly owned by The Library Association.

Except as otherwise permitted under the Copyright Designs and Patents Act 1988 this publication may only be reproduced, stored or transmitted in any form or by any means, with the prior permission of the publishers, or, in the case of reprographic reproduction, in accordance with the terms of a licence issued by The Copyright Licensing Agency. Enquiries concerning reproduction outside those terms should be sent to Library Association Publishing, 7 Ridgmount Street, London WC1E 7AE.

First published 1998

British Library Cataloguing in Publication Data.
A catalogue record for this book is available from the British Library.

ISBN 1-85604-256-1

Typeset in 11/12pt Palermo from author's disk by Library Association Publishing
Printed and made in Great Britain by The LooseLeaf Company, Midsomer Norton, Somerset

Contents

Acknowledgments	ix
1 Introduction	1
2 Change – theories, strategy and implementation	3
3 The role of training and development in achieving change	12
4 Change and the individual	14
5 Communication	18
6 Involving people	22
7 Group development	24
8 Skills training	29
9 Working with resistance to change	31
10 Change agents	35
11 Creating the future	38
Select bibliography	40
Examples Sample working documents	42
Index	61

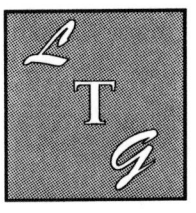 # Acknowledgments

This training guide is a product of my experience of life, and in particular of working with many people in many organizations. In recent years most of my working life has been spent helping individuals, groups and organizations achieve useful change. Each such occasion has given me an opportunity to learn. Often I have been challenged to the extent that I have arrived at a new understanding. I am grateful to all those who have helped provide these opportunities for my learning.

However regarding this guide I specifically wish to thank a number of people and they are: Jan Adams, Anne Bell, Sue Clegg, Sheila Corrall, Brian Gambles, Mike Heery, Grace Kempster, Philip Lewer, Tricia Little, Moira McLaughlin, Pat Noon, Jo Orange, Liz Roberts and Roy Williams. When the guide was being researched and written they helped me in various ways, which included sharing ideas and experience, providing me with documents, making constructive critical comments and giving me encouragement.

There are three other people I also wish to thank. David Baker for identifying that I had the ability to write a previous Library Training Guide, *Management of training and staff development*. The success of that guide gave me confidence to tackle this one. The trust and encouragement I have received from David Baker and from Joan Welsby have been invaluable to me. Finally I thank Arthur Whetherly for his support and his certainty that the guide could and would be written.

June Whetherly

1 Introduction

'Achieving change?': why use this title? The intention of the guide is to focus on the training and development facets of managing change. It does not set out to be a 'how to manage change' book, though it will overlap with such a text. Successfully managing the human aspects of change, a significant component of which is training and development, is likely to be central to achieving any useful change.

Research undertaken in preparation for writing this guide revealed that the phrases *managing change* and *managing organizational change* have different and sometimes contradictory meanings, depending on who is asked for his or her opinion. Some authors would question whether the types of change listed in the next sentence constitute *improvement* or *change*, or for that matter whether fundamental shifts in organizations can be managed.[1] This guide will focus on achieving changes such as restructuring, introducing new services, altering opening hours, changing the organization's culture and creating an environment in which people are ready for constant change.

However as organizations are made up of people with individual needs and aspirations, it is necessary to look at change as experienced by individuals and groups. The text will not focus on 'personal' development, though paradoxically it will look at how individual development can aid organizational development.

Chapter 2 is a brief overview of strategic approaches to managing change, and concludes there is no 'right' model of change that has universal application.

However, when it comes to implementing change there appears to be some consensus. Plant[2] suggests six key activities for successful implementation which provide a framework for exploring the role of training and staff development in achieving change.

In most organizations, some people will have a positive attitude to change. They might also possess the appropriate skills and knowledge of the change agent. Others may need help to acquire such qualities. Chapter 10 will explore this further.

Can an organization help itself to become capable of continuous change? The notion of the learning organization (see Chapter 11) suggests that staff who know how to learn, who are committed to learning and to using their learning, are more likely to spot the potential for useful change in their organization.

Successfully managing change is a complex process that can bring great satisfaction. It can also be a frustrating and stressful experience. It is hoped that this guide will enhance the capacity of change agents to achieve useful change.

> Sometimes it is easier to illuminate a point by drawing on individual experience. Any text in a framed paragraph falls into this category.
>
> It seems appropriate to set out my 'starting' point. Since 1990 my main work has been facilitating the learning of individuals and groups to achieve change. As an independent consultant mainly working in the library and information science (LIS) field, I am involved in individual, group and organizational change facilitation, for example counselling/coaching individuals, awaydays for senior management, team building/development for groups, customer care programmes for whole LIS departments.
>
> Previously I worked for 25 years, latterly as a senior manager, in public libraries. I have come to realize that I have a tendency to need to sort out 'how will it be done' and pay less attention to strategy. With the benefit of hindsight, I can appreciate that 10 years ago I would have managed change differently if for example I had applied my current knowledge about the open systems models to my role as a senior manager.

References

1. Critchley, B., 'The myth of managing change', *Leadership and organization development journal*, **17** (2), 1996, 48–52.
2. Plant, R., *Managing change and making it stick*, London, Fontana, 1987.

Change – theories, strategy and implementation

2.1 Introduction

Organizational change is complex. Many theories and approaches exist, often offered as 'the answer' to managing change. This chapter provides a very brief overview of some theories and ideas about change, in the belief that 'there is nothing so practical as a good theory'.

2.2 Schools of change management theory

It has been suggested that change management is not a distinct discipline. Instead Burnes[1] puts forward the idea that it draws on a number of social science disciplines. He suggests that the three schools of thought that underpin change management theory are:

- the individual perspective school
- the group dynamics school
- the open systems school.

Very brief summaries of each school follow. For each, examples are given to indicate how the theory might be applied in the context of training and development.

2.3 Individual perspective school

The individual perspective school can be split into two camps, the behaviourists and the gestalt psychologists. Both provide insight into how individuals have potential to change given the appropriate environment.

2.3.1 Behaviourists

Behaviourists believe that behaviour is learned and results from the interaction of an individual with his or her environment. For example the behaviourist B. F. Skinner worked on the significance of reinforcement as a way of influencing behaviour. Straight after the behaviour in question, a reinforcer, which can be positive or negative, encourages the behaviour to recur. A supervisor, who repeatedly succeeds in persuading a member of staff to undertake a task after having asked for its completion several times, is positively reinforced to behave similarly in future, and the member of staff is similarly reinforced to undertake the task after being asked several times.

Honey,[2] who describes how his approach to solving people problems utilizes behaviourist theory, gives an example of how positive reinforcement might operate to achieve punctuality. If someone regularly comes to work about 30 minutes late, initially reinforce the latecomer only when 25 minutes late. As progress is made, successively reduce this by 5 minutes to 20, 15 minutes, etc. until eventually reinforcement only takes place when the person is on time or even early. Honey does not indicate what the reinforcer might be, though presumably it could be a cheery 'good morning'.

2.3.2 Gestalt psychologists

Gestalt psychologists consider that in addition to interaction with the environment, behaviour is also a product of thinking, leading to increased awareness of self and individual insight. 'The Gestalt therapy view sees the healthy person very much as a whole organism, an organism in constant and dynamic relationship with her environment.'[3]

Houston, a gestalt practitioner, writes:

> Fritz Perls, the originator of gestalt therapy, often said that gestalt is the psychology of the obvious. He believed that we can very effectively learn ourselves, and learn our best ways of dealing with ourselves, each other and the world, by becoming more and more aware of what stands out for us from moment to moment right here in the present.[4]

An example of applying the gestalt approach is of the members of a work group setting out to improve how they function as a team. A workshop attended by group members uses an exercise that asks each of them to imagine they are in, or by the side of, a swimming pool, or on the diving board. They are to stand up and place themselves in the location that feels right for them as they experience themselves in the team. A fairly new member initially locates her or himself coming out of the changing room, having not yet tested the water. An outcome for this person, having felt how uncomfortable it is in the changing room, could be an action plan to achieve greater integration into the team, which would enable him or her to get into the water.

2.4 Group dynamics school

Theories of group dynamics are concerned with the nature of groups and of their development. Each group can be seen to have its own patterns of interaction and characteristics – a life of its own. For instance, it will have group norms that determine how people in the group should behave in certain situations. An example of a group norm is the understanding, without its ever having been discussed, that everyone will stay on for an extra hour or two to get the job completed.

The significance of such theories for change management is that in organizations workers operate in groups, and effective team working is generally regarded to be important. By analysing and understanding the *process* of the group an intended outcome is the mature, performing team. Process refers to the

> interaction, feelings and relationships that exist in any group between its members. Some of these are explicit, some barely perceived and some, deriving as they do from the unconscious, are not usually recognised at all - at least at the time. Process is about affection and alliances at the one end, and conflict and animosity at the other.[5]

Put another way, 'it is the technical name for all the subtle shifting of power, of comfort, of dissatisfaction, of warmth and so on',[6] that goes on in groups.

Used with a different emphasis, the swimming pool exercise can facilitate greater understanding of the group dynamics operating within the team. A group can use it as a tool to identify process issues that might be blocking the performance of the team. For example, is there anything about the norms of the team that leads to one person steadfastly staying in the changing room? Is this team member feeling under considerable pressure to stay on to finish the job, knowing that there is a conflict with domestic responsibilities? Can or should anything be done to change the norms?

2.5 Open systems schools

The third school refers to the whole organization. Organizations do not operate in isolation from the rest of the world. To assume they did would suggest they could be regarded as closed systems that can survive on their own.

Equally, individual departments are not closed but can be regarded as subsystems that are connected. What happens in one subsystem will affect another. For example, if a university registrar introduces a 'smart card', which enables access for the holder to all appropriate services and departments, this will have significance for the library service.

Figure 2.1 relates one open system model to an imaginary public library, a subsystem of a local authority.

Because the open system approach looks at the whole organization, it has been suggested that it has the following implications for achieving change.[7] Firstly, if change takes place in one interdependent subsystem without regard to the others, the outcome may be less satisfactory. The successful introduction of a smart card by one department will require consultation with other parts of an organization.

The second implication, which is particularly relevant to this text, is that on its own training is unlikely to succeed as a mechanism for change. Training can lead to individual change that may in turn lead to organizational change, though this is not guaranteed. Providing customer care training for everyone in the service will, it is hoped, lead to fewer complaints. However, if staff perceive that the will to improve other aspects of the service, such as access, does not exist, such change is likely to be undermined.

A third implication is that the organization needs fully to engage the energy and skills of the staff. As a consequence, structures, organization norms and reward systems may need to be altered to achieve this degree of engagement. Alterations can be simple, such as ensuring people are thanked for their contributions, or more significant, as when work structures are altered fully to utilize skills in the department.

> Many years ago, as an Area Librarian, I tried to manage the area service as though it was a closed system. This would have been doomed to failure had I not begun to realize I was paying insufficient attention to significant influences and factors beyond the area, which could have led to missed opportunities and undetected threats.

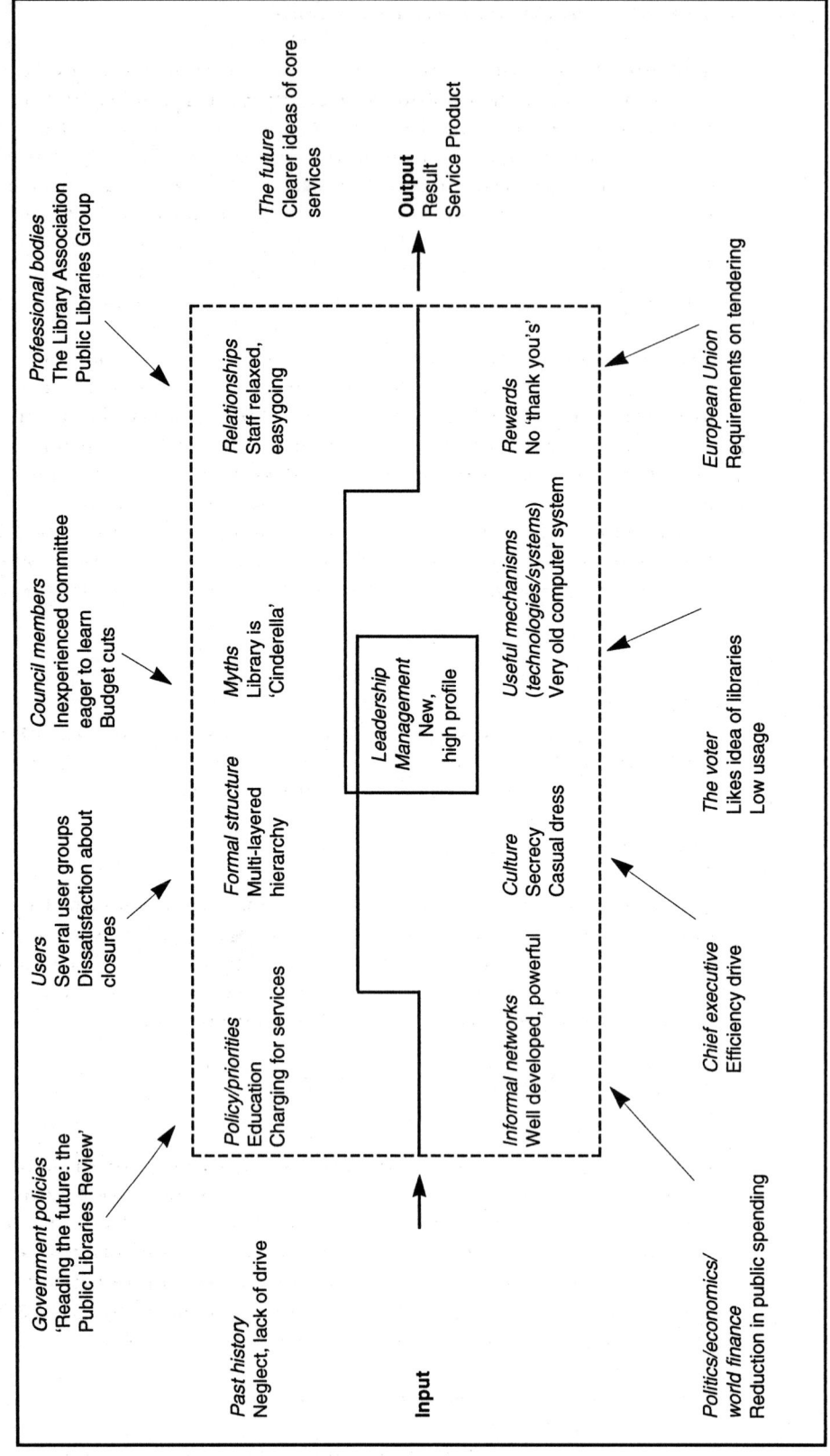

Fig. 2.1 *Open system model: applied to an imaginary UK public library*

2.6 The three schools: how they relate

Though it can appear that each of these schools is offered as the 'most effective' approach to achieving change, they can be seen to offer complementary approaches. This view relates to the paradox referred to in the Introduction. Organizations comprise people and groups, and it is their effort that enables organizational change to occur. Also it is quite likely that all approaches could be in use in an organization at the same time.

It is also possible that a manager favouring one perspective will overlook the potential of the others. For example, a librarian who understands and appreciates the significance of group dynamics might focus attention on the management team he or she leads, on the assumption that if the team works effectively it will be able to take the service forward. The result may be to overlook the wider context within which the department operates or the need to coach one individual fully to contribute to the team.

The complexity of change management is well summarized by Wilson.[8] 'The danger lies in assuming change to be a simple phenomenon, attached as a sub-theme to organizational behaviour and manageable through a finite list of behavioural recipes and managerial competences. The study of organizational change requires an interdisciplinary focus which allows an appreciation of the contexts in which strategies for change are conceived and enacted.'

2.7 Other ideas on change management

In addition to the theories referred to above, there are other approaches and models that underpin the development of strategies for managing change. This section looks at three topical areas.

2.7.1 Planned and/or emergent change

Currently much is written about planned and emergent change. *Planned* change has been described as an approach that 'views organisational change as essentially a process of moving from one fixed state to another through a series of predictable and pre-planned steps'.[9] The classic example of this approach is Kurt Lewin's three-step model:

1 unfreezing the current level of performance
2 moving to a new level
3 refreezing at the new level.

In contrast, *emergent* change 'starts from the assumption that change is a continuous, open-ended and unpredictable process of aligning and realigning an organization to its changing environment'.[10] The open system models provide a tool for taking a snapshot of this environment at any given time. They can also enable the potential for change to be identified. For example, changes in government policy and user expectations can be used as a starting point for a review of the existing service.

2.7.2 Improvement or fundamental change

Another view is that a distinction can be drawn between improvement and fundamental change. Doing things better can be regarded as *improvement*, whereas change that is *fundamental* involves shifts in deeply held assumptions about an organization and of the nature of organizations. Critchley[11] proposes that methods and techniques designed to lead to improvement, such as total quality management, are not applicable to achieving fundamental change. The latter would apply when, for example, an organization seeks to change its culture. A library example of culture change is a move from holding stock intended to be a representative selection of the best titles available to a collection that reflects only user demand, or vice versa. Whilst Critchley does not link improvement with planned change and a fundamental shift with emergent change, such an association of ideas seems relevant.

2.7.3 *Turbulence*

There is also much talk of the 'turbulent times' in which we exist. In the context of change, *turbulence* is used to describe 'an environment characterized both by several changes occurring rapidly and simultaneously and by a situation such that only the most optimistic see the possibility of a return to a more stable environment in the foreseeable future'.[12] In these conditions the emergent approach appears to be most relevant.

Whichever labels and models are preferred, as pointed out above more than one approach may be operating in the same organization simultaneously. For example, a library service may, as part of the overall organization strategy, be systematically introducing an appraisal scheme, whilst constantly reviewing the impact of information technology because new user demands and products appear every day. One library practitioner, Corrall,[13] cautions against abandoning planned change whilst still recognizing the importance of emergent change.

2.8 The context in which organizational change takes place

Typically, any of a number of triggers can set off change. For example, a reduction or increase in budget, a new vice-chancellor or head of department, or a significant development in information technology. When it is recognized that change needs to occur, knowledge of theories and models of change can enable and inform choice of strategies. A new manager faced with a moribund service might decide to restructure it using a planned approach with a completion date targeted within one year, in the hope that this will provide a necessary shake-up. Every effort is made to develop all staff to undertake new roles. Associated with the restructuring is a clear set of ideas about the purpose of the service. As part of a longer-term strategy that manager may also decide to try to create a climate in which staff feel able to try out new ideas, learn new skills and participate more in decision-making processes.

However, a theoretical underpinning must be accompanied by an understanding of the organization's particular situation. For each organization there will be a set of circumstances that will both have an impact on choice of strategy and be affected by the strategies adopted.

Consider staff attitudes to change. If in the past staff have experienced change as positive and the climate of the organization leads them to feel valued, they are more likely to embrace new change. Where the opposite exists, and change is seen as negative, part of a change strategy might well be to seek to reverse these attitudes. As a result, all staff might be involved in workshops on change and the individual, to provide them with insight into the processes of change. They may also be asked to attend forums to contribute to working out how to achieve necessary change. In addition a training need for some managers may be the acquisition of the necessary interpersonal skills (see Chapter 10).

The next section looks at some of the local circumstances likely to have a bearing on choice of strategies.

2.8.1 Circumstances that affect choice of change strategies

The need for change

There are three main categories:

- change of purpose: e.g. a public library that decides its primary reason for existing is information provision and the support of education, through whichever medium is appropriate, fully utilizing IT (rather than focusing on lending books for leisure reading)
- change of strategy: e.g. a library that moves from highly centralized control of finances to a series of cost centres
- improvement to the effectiveness of the organization: e.g. working towards and applying for Investors in People (a nationally recognized standard in the UK designed to enable employers to develop employees, and the organization, alongside clear business objectives).

Magnitude of change

This can range from minor timetable alterations to a company take-over and relocation leading to redundancies as two information services are merged.

Time-scales

Sometimes organizational change is required urgently, though practitioners warn against forcing the plant in the greenhouse only for it to perish outside. It has been suggested that if in the past change has been experienced as positive, it may be possible to proceed more quickly at times of crisis. Significant change can take years. John Harvey-Jones[14] suggests that on average five years are needed for changing attitudes.

Past experiences of change in the organization

These can vary, leading staff to expect change and understand that it is essential to survival or to anticipate it will be mishandled and something to be feared.

Knowledge and skills base of staff

Staff who have insight into change processes, and are skilled learners, are likely to live more easily with change than those who do not possess such attributes. These notions are explored further in Chapter 4.

Change in the subsystem and/or the whole organization

A library or information service, for example, may be introducing a new computer system to improve efficiency, at the same time as the parent organization is attempting to empower staff by undertaking a programme of wider change, including shifting control of budgets to those delivering services.

Proactive or reactive change

Probably most change management is reactive, triggered, for example, by different levels of resourcing. Sometimes positive action is taken to review services when no obvious driver of change is apparent.

2.9 Implementing change

Theoretical knowledge can usefully underpin the development of a strategy that takes into account the circumstances of the particular organization. However, as was suggested earlier, organizational change is complex and not a simple phenomenon. For this reason this text does not propose that there is one 'right' model or theory of change that has universal application.

In contrast, when it comes to the practicalities of implementing change rather than developing a strategy, there appears to be a considerable amount of agreement as to the best methods. Preparatory research for this guide, in the form of interviews with practitioners, reading the literature, and the author's own experience, suggests there are several key activities. These are summarized by Plant:[15]

- providing help to individuals and groups to face up to change
- communicating to a greater extent than before
- gaining energetic commitment to change
- involving people early in the formulation of change
- creating positive perceptions of change as an opportunity not threat
- avoiding over-organizing and planning down to the last detail.

This list contributes to a framework for looking at the role of training and staff development in achieving change, which is explored in the following chapters.

This chapter sets out to:

- introduce briefly some theories and models applicable to change management, which relate to the individual, the group and the organization
- identify other factors that affect choice of strategy
- note characteristics common to the successful implementation of change.

References

1 Burnes, B., *Managing change: a strategic approach to organisational dynamics*, 2nd edn, London, Pitman, 1996, 173.
2 Honey, P., *Solving people problems*, London, McGraw Hill, 1980, 75.
3 Ernst, S. and Goodison, L., *In our own hands: a book of self-help therapy*, London, Women's Press, 1981, 58.
4 Houston, G., *The red book of gestalt*, 5th rev. edn, London, Rochester Foundation, 1990, 10.
5 Gaunt, R., *Personal and group development for managers: an integrated*

approach through action learning, Harlow, Longman, 1991, 67.
6 Houston, op. cit., 43.
7 Burnes, op. cit., 178.
8 Wilson, D., *A strategy of change: concepts and controversies in the management of change*, London, Routledge, 1992, 129.
9 Burnes, op. cit., 170.
10 Ibid.
11 Critchley, B., 'The myth of managing change', *Leadership and organization development journal*, **17** (2), 1996.
12 Sadler, P., *Managing change*, London, Kogan Page, 1995, 21.
13 Corrall, S., Dempsey, L., Law, D. and Mowat, I. (eds.), 'An evolving service: managing change', in *Networking and the future of libraries 2: managing the intellectual record: an international conference held at the University of Bath, 19–21 April 1995*, London, Library Association Publishing, 1995, 58.
14 Harvey-Jones, J., *Making it happen: reflections on leadership*, London, Fontana, 1988, 147.
15 Plant, R., *Managing change and making it stick*, London, Fontana, 1987, 32–4.

3 The role of training and development in achieving change

Training and development are here defined to include creating any opportunity for learning that helps to facilitate the process of achieving change. A casual conversation with the head of service in which the vision of what is to be achieved is further explained, formal briefing sessions and written newsletters, workshops about the theory of change, team building for a new team, and specific skills training are all examples.

Such a wide definition begs the question of what type of training/development intervention is necessary to achieve a particular change? Figure 3.1 provides a model, based on the work of Stewart,[1] who argues that for individuals to change their behaviour, learning needs to occur and motivation to exist to enable the learning to be applied. He also suggests[2] that the *results* of learning are *knowledge*, *skills* and *values/attitudes*, though the final outcome is behaviour. It is changed *behaviour* that is sought by making any intervention.

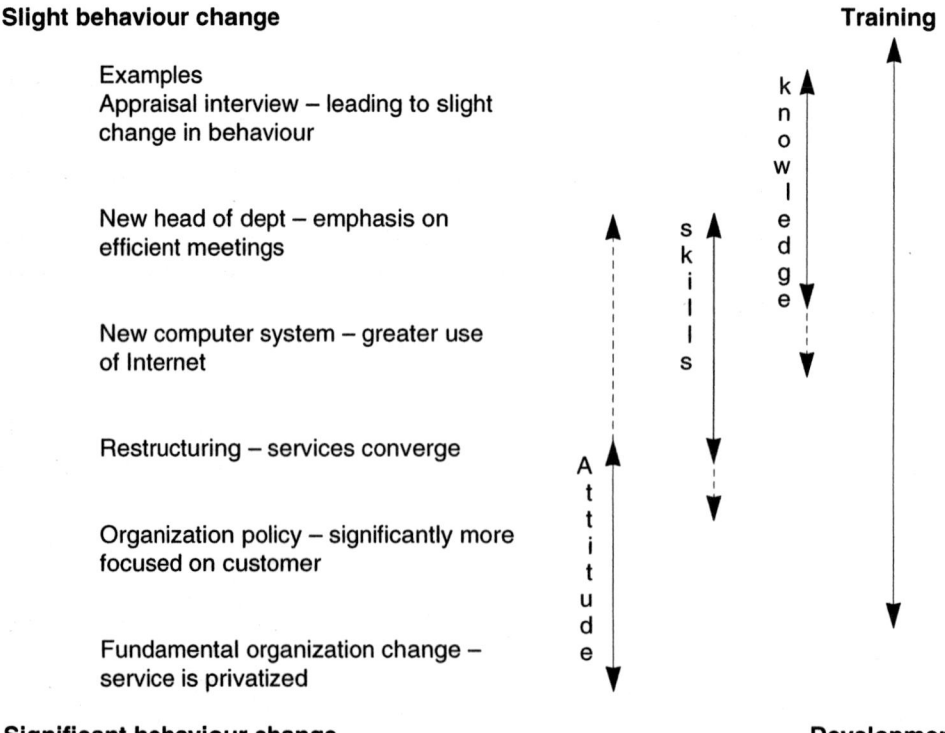

Fig. 3.1 *Individual behaviour change and training and development*

3.1 Changes in behaviour

In terms of achieving organizational change, it seems appropriate to use the measure of changed behaviour as a sign that learning has taken place. To take an example from Figure 3.1, a new head of department considers that there is a need for more efficient and effective meetings. After various interventions intended to aid learning, behaviour changes exhibited among attendees of the regular meeting are:

- agenda items sent in good time to the chair (previously left to chair to chase up)
- advance preparation demonstrated by knowledge of topics for discussion (items no longer constantly deferred)
- all participants contribute as relevant (in the past the views of a few people were dominant)
- punctual and regular attendance
- smiles and laughter (rather than all gloom and doom).

Interventions that contributed to these changes included:

- the new head of department expressed concerns about the meetings
- attendees and the chair explored what helped and hindered
- agreement was reached on how to conduct the meetings
- some participants, including the chair, received training on 'meeting skills'.

Drawing on the model in Fig 3.1, knowledge and skills are key areas of learning. Knowledge of meetings and how they can be conducted, helped lead to changed behaviour, as did learning new 'meeting' skills. It may be that for some or all of the people involved attitudes and values were also significant: if a participant has little faith in the value of the meetings, will new knowledge of the potential of the meetings be sufficient to change that attitude?

The question just posed indicates that rigid adherence to this model is inadvisable. However, it can be a useful tool for considering what degree of behaviour change is involved and what needs to be learned. This will vary from person to person, as will how each person seeks out or responds to change.

This chapter has:

- defined the terms training and development as used in this text
- introduced a model for individual behaviour change and training and development.

References

1. Stewart, J., *Managing change through training and development*, London, Kogan Page, 1991, 205.
2. Stewart, J., 'Towards a model of HRD', *Training and development*, **10** (10), Oct. 1992, 26–9.

# Change and the individual

4.1 Facing up to change

Our individual responses to change vary considerably. Past personal experience at home and work, how we feel about ourselves, the support structures we have in place in or out of the workplace, and our beliefs about how change happens will all have an impact.

Change as experienced by the individual can be associated with loss. For example, taking on a new role in a restructured service, no matter how exciting for the person in question, will mean giving up a former role. If this change is perceived as denying the opportunity to practise skills learnt over many years, the loss will be much greater. When a person is keen to embrace the new role, the sense of loss may be fleeting or imperceptible. For others it may feel devastating.

Loss can be associated with the stages experienced in bereavement. Jacobs[1] notes the possible stages, listed in the left-hand column of Table 4.1. Instead of the phrases associated with grieving that Jacobs used, in the right-hand column common reactions heard at the time of an organizational restructuring are given. However, it is important to remember that people are different and not everyone will feel the same.

Table 4.1 *Change and the individual*

Stages of bereavement	Possible reactions to a **restructuring** within the organization
Shock	I couldn't think straight when I heard about it
Numbness and unreality	Tell me again
Disbelief	It can't be true
Yearning	I wish the service was like it used to be
Emptiness	All I've worked for will be thrown away
Searching	Can't we find another way around this problem?
Anxiety	Will I lose my job?
Anger	They have no right to reorganize the service again so soon
Guilt	If only I had . . .
Remembering	I shall forget what it used to be like
Depression	I'm too tired to bother
Loss of identity and status	Who am I?
Stigma	I'm an embarrassment to others
Loss of faith	Why?
Loneliness	I shall miss working with . . .
Acceptance	If Joan was still here she'd laugh about all that has been going on
Healing	I can see this new structure will have some advantages

CHANGE AND THE INDIVIDUAL

Ideas underpinned by such knowledge of how we experience loss are increasingly used in management and staff development to aid understanding of how change may be experienced by an individual. They are often represented as a transition curve: see Figure 4.1.

4.2 The transition curve

The equivalent of a bereavement, in terms of what happens in the organization at the start of the curve, might be the arrival of a new line manager with a very different approach, the introduction of a computer system using the World Wide Web or a restructuring programme. If the change is seen to be negative or was not predicted, shock is likely to be experienced. This can lead people to feel overwhelmed, and unable to reason or plan. Patience, listening and encouragement are likely to be needed in the face of the self-doubt, anxiety and uncertainty felt.

The next stage can lead to euphoria – 'at last we can get going on this project' – or denial – 'it won't happen; they are always coming up with these grand ideas'. This can be a key time for resistance to what is seen as unwelcome change. In library and information services, this has led to card catalogues being maintained unofficially alongside the computerized records designed to replace them. The new 'reality' has not fully replaced the old. Communication and strong role models are likely to be vital. Those in leadership roles will be going through their own transition in addition to helping others, though if the change is planned, they may well be a few stages ahead, having been involved earlier.

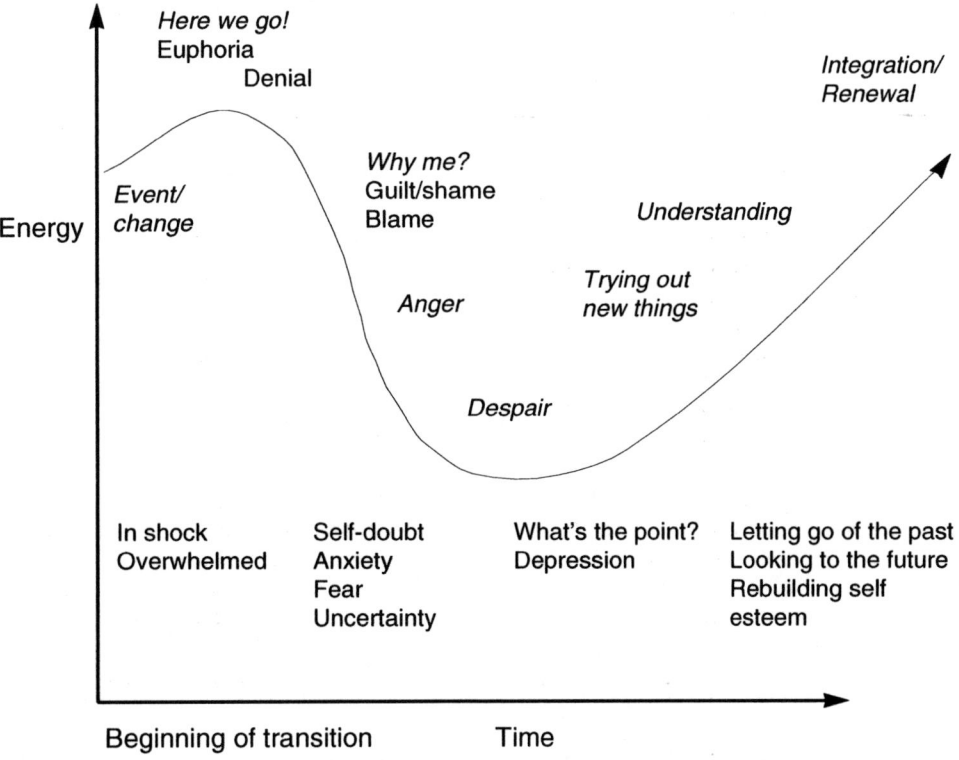

Fig. 4.1 *A transition curve*

Feelings such as guilt, anger and despair, experienced as individuals concentrate on the impact of the changes on themselves, can fuel resistance. It will probably be a difficult time requiring, in response, empathy, the acknowledgement of those feelings and the sense of loss. The doubts and fears staff experience will need to be listened to and each person encouraged to identify at least small steps forward.

'Counselling' is likely to give way to mentoring as new practices and roles are tried out. As they become more familiar, time for reflection will enable each person to search for meaning, that is, an understanding of the changes that have been gone through. Eventually the changes will be fully internalized and integrated.

As described here, it sounds as though people smoothly move through a series of stages. This may be the case, but often transition is experienced as one step forward, two steps back. To let go of the past and move to the future, while living in the present, is not easy for most people. For some it may be tremendously difficult. The story of the executive who continues to commute to work, not having told the family that her or his post has been made redundant, is a good example.

4.3 Helping people face up to change

In describing how people may be helped to work through the transition curve, it becomes apparent that each person must be treated as an individual who will bring different experiences, knowledge and attitudes to the change currently occurring.

Appropriate approaches and responses to individuals can be supplemented by helping them to learn about change. It can be useful for staff to have knowledge and understanding of:

- models of change, for example open systems models and the transition curve
- how they and others experience change
- their attitudes to change
- what changes are affecting their organization.

For example, the author has found that most people quickly appreciate the significance of the transition curve. They find it reassuring to know that working through the stages is a natural and normal response. It helps explain why they can experience a range of emotions, some of which are difficult or uncomfortable, and that not everyone responds to an organizational change in the same way.

A typical way of meeting such learning needs is the provision of workshops. The content of these will vary and may set out to cover any of the elements listed above. If particular attention is to be paid to current organizational change, workshops are often undertaken in-house. Examples of training and developmental methods used are:

- exercises to enable greater understanding of individual responses to change
  - individuals draw what 'change' means to them, and then discuss the drawing with a colleague
  - in pairs, participants consider what helped them to take part in change and what led them to want to resist change
  - after such exercises, the experiences of the whole group are drawn

out and shared, and theoretical models may be introduced
- theory input – the transition curve is explained to the group
- application of theory
  - participants are asked to 'draw' their workplace using the open system model, then discuss what they have recorded
  - as a result, what potential for useful change can they identify?
- facilitating change in the organization
  - in pairs, participants describe how they feel about the current change
  - the group works on opportunities/concerns about the changes.

4.4 The role and development of managers

Managers, in addition to the above, can benefit by having:

- an understanding of the processes of change
- an ability to help people engage and come to terms with change.

Increasingly, change management is included in management development and training. There is evidence that such provision is being made in formal courses, provided in the library and information services sector.

There are various ways of enhancing management development besides formal courses. Examples are guided reading to increase understanding of change management, being coached while introducing a change to the service, and working in a problem solving group, such as an action learning set,[2] which additionally leads to increased self-knowledge and awareness. In-house courses and workshops may be specifically targeted to the needs of managers. Change that is across the whole organization provides developmental opportunities for learning with colleagues from other departments. Generally, learning is facilitated if it can be seen to be relevant. For this reason, in-house training and development on change management are most likely to be associated with achieving changes currently being sought.

To help others engage with change, it is likely to be necessary that the manager's own response to change has been explored and understood. In addition the 'change agent' needs certain skills: see Chapter 10.

This chapter has:

- identified how change can be experienced as loss by the individual
- introduced the transition curve
- explored how individuals can be helped to face up to change by
  - responding appropriately to the individual, managers in particular
  - outlining the contribution of training and development.

References

1. Jacobs, M., *The presenting past: an introduction to practical psychodynamic counselling*, Milton Keynes, Open University Press, 1985, 200–1.
2. Whetherly, J., 'Action learning: developing the person and the organisation', *Personnel, training and education: a journal for library and information workers*, **13** (2), September 1996, 3–5.

5 Communication

5.1 Introduction

Communicate, communicate, communicate. Writers on change management emphasize the importance of communication, and some practitioners suggest that it is unlikely that even the most energetic of managers will ever communicate sufficiently. So why bother? A fundamental reason is to show respect to all the stakeholders of change. A likely outcome is that people will be more responsive to change.

Communication is important in order to establish the need for change, to convey ideas and to obtain feedback by encouraging people to express their opinions or objections. It is a two-way process that provides a key method of involving people. Aiming for good communication is desirable at all times. However, it is especially important in the early stages of organizational change. As one practitioner said, 'if the 'why' [make the changes] is not clear, you are struggling all the time'.

Formal and informal communication happens in all organizations. One way in which communication can be achieved is on the grapevine. It is often said that information will spread more quickly this way than through official channels. However, reliance on the grapevine or an assumption that information will reach people this way is likely to lead to the dissemination of distorted versions of the truth, leading to unhelpful rumour and gossip.

5.2 How to communicate

There are many methods open to change agents, some of which are noted below.

Examples of written communication are:

- newsletters
- a statement of the vision behind the change
- surveys of staff opinion
- letters
- plans for change, such as how the new departmental structure might look
- an open wall on which all staff can post ideas.

Examples of verbal communication include:

- a meeting of the whole department
- change-project group meetings
- casual conversations in the corridor
- one to one meetings, formal or informal.

Today the development of technology means that there are many choices available. For example one to one written communication could take the following forms:

- word-processed letter
- handwritten note
- faxed version of either of the above
- e-mail message.

5.3 Qualities of effective communication

Perhaps top of the list of qualities is *clarity* about what is to be written or said. Useful questions that the originators of information can ask themselves are 'Why is this information needed?' and 'How will it be used?'. Take the example of a head of department setting out proposals for restructuring a service. He or she may decide it is essential to indicate the threats associated with making or not making changes, as well as the opportunities and benefits. This information is perceived as necessary to inform and engage staff in working out how to proceed in the context of ensuring that the service develops. By being open and honest about both the opportunities and threats and by anticipating some of the issues that may cause concern, the head of department's intention is to encourage trust and acceptance of the proposal as a sound starting point that generates feedback and ideas.

In addition to clarity, *open* and *honest* approaches aid communication. Openness involves both giving information and being ready to be challenged by those holding other viewpoints. Conveying a *consistent* message, which is *correct* and in *clear language*, is also important. The choice of words can have a significant effect on outcomes. Recently the term appraisal has been linked with processes to achieve different objectives, ranging from identifying individual development needs, to determining organizational training needs, through to assessing performance to establish levels of remuneration. Often there has been unease when it was introduced because it was unclear to staff what was meant by 'appraisal'. Phrases such as 'staff development interviews' have been used as an alternative when the focus is on identifying training and development needs.

Judging how much information is *sufficient* is not easy. There may be complaints that 'nobody told me anything about that'. These may indeed be justified, yet they can also be the result of information overload, which can cause individuals to filter out subsequently important items that do not seem relevant at the time.

The qualities identified apply to written and verbal communication. In addition verbal communication affords the opportunity for immediate interaction. The concerns, issues and other responses of all participants can be *listened to, acknowledged* and *noted*. The spoken word will not be the only source of information about people's thoughts and feelings. *Non-verbal messages* will also be available: the person who stands up at a meeting and jabs a pointed finger in the direction of the last speaker is probably angry.

5.4 Choice of method

At the beginning of this chapter it was suggested that communication is never likely to be sufficient to meet all needs. One way of addressing this problem is to convey the same information using at least three different methods.[1] For example, in addition to an announcement being made at a meeting attended by all staff, individual memos are sent to all people affected, who are also invited to attend a one-to-one meeting to ensure they are fully informed and have the opportunity to express their concerns and issues.

One of the reasons for not relying on one method, such as a general memo to all staff, is that there is no guarantee that all recipients will read and understand the document. In addition, if the document is not addressed to all people individually, some may not receive a copy. In organizations with a hierarchical structure, this problem may be compounded if managers decide who they think should receive copies rather than ensuring the distribution includes everyone.

It is also important to pay attention to the existence of informal networks. Power and influence in organizations are not only exercised through formal networks such as these represented by the organization structure chart. Alternative and informal networks exist. For example, 'membership' might comprise those who have lunch together, go for a drink after work, share a cigarette break or sit together in the staff room. These networks are also dependent on the layout and geography of the department.

Informal networks can have a significant impact on the way the department or organization operates. This suggests that it is important to consider whether and how to involve informal networks appropriately in the communication process. An example of how informal networks can influence outcomes relates to a customer care training programme all staff are required to attend. Initially it is met with scepticism, but by the time a couple of groups have attended the workshop and found it useful, this positive response becomes known throughout the department. In consequence later groups respond quite differently. They expect to find the day useful and do not show the considerable resistance noticed in the first groups.

5.5 The time to communicate

People involved in change management talk about *timeliness*. However, it is difficult to determine when to engage in timely communication. It might seem obvious to present plans to staff, before taking them to the parent organization, in order to avoid instant alienation of staff to proposals. Yet how does the change agent judge the right time to present the plans in the first place? When asked, practitioners have said they pick up nuances of feeling and use their intuition, and that it is a matter of taking opportunities as presented. One reason that organizational change so often follows the appointment of a new head of service is the presence of such opportunity or even an expectation that change will occur.

Another factor to consider is the *frequency* of communication. It is important to keep information flowing and to make it available when needed. Time needs to be allowed for the individual to absorb information and make sense of it. This relates to the way people experience change as described in the last chapter.

5.6 Who is involved in the communication process?

Key members of staff are those managing the change process. They have a particular responsibility to allocate time to think through what information needs to be communicated, as well as to talk with stakeholders (all those who have an interest in the changes) and provide written material.

It is essential for organizational change projects that the head of service is actively involved or supportive of the changes. In an organization embarking on a customer care programme, the head of service could be directly involved as project leader. Alternatively that role might be delegated. However, to ensure that the importance placed on the programme is apparent to all, the programme might be on every agenda of the management team, and no action or decision making allowed that would contradict the stated priority of the scheme. In addition the impact of the programme will probably be greater if the head of service attends workshops provided for all staff.

However, it is not only managers who are involved. All stakeholders need to be engaged in the communication process. The staff are a significant group of stakeholders. Depending on the change, staff in other departments, service users and the board of management might also be included. Applying the open system model referred to in Chapter 2 can help to clarify who the stakeholders are in any given situation.

Clarity about who the stakeholders are can also help the change managers to anticipate the professional and technical issues and concerns each group might have. For example a key group could be the children's librarians who fear their specialism will be lost in the change to team-based working.

This chapter has explored:

- why the emphasis on communication is well placed
- effective ways of communicating
- who is involved and when they need to communicate.

Reference

1 O'Connor, C. A., *The handbook for organizational change: strategy and skill for trainers and developers*, London, McGraw-Hill, 1993, 70.

# Involving people

6.1 Why involve people?

There are many reasons for doing so. Involvement:

- encourages 'ownership' of the change leading to commitment
- can reduce resistance to change
- helps establish all the options to achieve the 'vision'
- means respecting the value everyone can add
- can ensure the history of the service/organization is taken into account, not denied
- means the workload can be shared
- allows detailed planning and practical matters to be dealt with by those with the relevant experience
- provides ongoing developmental opportunities to expand horizons and learn skills.

Probably the most significant issue addressed by involving people fully in the change process is gaining commitment. This in turn is likely to lead to reduced resistance, a topic that will be explored further in Chapter 9. People who understand why the change is occurring and who are encouraged to affect the outcome are more likely to be committed. The change will be seen by them as being *their* change, rather than something imposed from above or elsewhere. For this reason it is important that past practice and experience are not disregarded, a strong temptation for the 'new broom'. Change may be needed, but if a service has survived it is highly unlikely that everything it did previously needs to be different.

Most of the reasons given above can be related to the change project in hand. Many organizations now consider that they need to create an environment in which people are ready for constant change, reflecting the pace of change in the wider world. Library and information services are particularly aware of the very rapid expansion and development of information technology. Taking a longer-term view, each experience of successfully managed change is likely to prepare staff for constant change. Also, each project has the potential to provide developmental opportunities, such as the chance to learn how to chair a meeting of a working party.

6.2 How to involve people

The last chapter explored communication. Effective communication is an essential tool for involving people throughout the change process. It is particularly important in the early stages.

In addition to the methods of communicating already referred to, the following list gives some activities that can be used to involve people:

- a survey providing the opportunity for individuals to state their views of the service
- a SWOT (strengths, weaknesses, opportunities and threats) analysis, for example on how the service is marketed
- open meetings to discuss the changes
- membership of a working party to write the specification of new equipment
- briefing sessions
- membership of a 'sounding board group' to act as change advisers to the senior management team
- visits to other library and information services to collect ideas
- the opportunity to hear guest speakers talking about their experiences of a similar change
- gathering information about the experiences of other services.

Given all the potential ways of involving people, care must be taken to ensure that the ongoing service is maintained. Many will be excited by the impending changes and can quickly put energy into achieving them to the neglect of the service. Seizing the moment will be important, though too many ad hoc arrangements might prove difficult to manage. Early on a strategic view on how to involve people is likely to prove helpful.

Style of leadership will also be very important. Exhorting others to communicate and involve people will be more effective if leaders are seen to practise what they preach. Such symbolism can have a powerful impact on the situation.

This chapter has identified:

- reasons why it is important to involve people
- some methods of involving staff.

 Group development

7.1 Why use groups?

One way of looking at an organization is to perceive it as an organism made up of individuals. However, this approach is incomplete, because in reality people within organizations come together in groups for a variety of reasons, both formal and informal. Many of the previously mentioned methods for ensuring good communication and involving people use groups.

Sometimes meetings take place of everyone within an organization or department. Such occasions often occur when major change in the organization is sought, and they provide an opportunity for everyone to hear the same message at the same time. They involve great investment of time, energy and money. However, a limitation is that by bringing together thousands or hundreds of people, it is difficult to actively involve participants. Meetings of smaller groups of staff provide a wide range of opportunities for change management.

7.2 Purposes and types of groups

There are many purposes groups can serve. Charles Handy[1] cites ten major reasons why organizations use groups all of which are relevant to organizational change. These include:

- work distribution
- management and control of work
- problem-solving
- decision-taking
- dissemination of information
- collecting ideas and information
- coordination and liaison between functions and divisions
- involving people
- resolution of conflict
- reviewing the past.

Groups may be temporary, or exist in the short or long term. Examples of temporary groups are when people come together for a one day workshop. Other groups may meet for a limited period of time, such as an IT group drawing up a specification for a new computer system, or a change project group advising senior management throughout a restructuring operation. Examples of groups existing in the long term include management, issue desk and customer service teams.

Defining the purpose or agenda of the group will need careful consideration, especially for those groups meeting for a limited period. Take a focus group set up to review the application of equal opportunities policies in the service, including the implications of the disability discrimination legislation. The group might be asked by a manager to look at service provision at the points of access, an interpretation of the agenda that might cause an incomplete picture to emerge. Alternatively, a totally free ranging exploration of the issues may lead to difficulty in identifying the significant and relevant points. This issue brings us directly onto consideration of group composition.

7.3 Group composition

Deciding who will be in a group is significant in terms of its progress and the outcomes. Should a SWOT analysis on how the library and information service is marketed be undertaken by self-selecting enthusiasts, who fully understand and appreciate the importance of marketing, by nominees thought by managers to need to develop such an approach, or a mixture of the two? A possible outcome is that the enthusiasts will be perceived as overlooking any difficulties marketing may present and to represent a partial view, while the nominees may resent time spent on such an activity and consciously or unconsciously set out to sabotage the group.

Probably the key factor in deciding group membership is whether people are involved voluntarily or not. A volunteer who is sceptical about marketing may add much value to the group by challenging other viewpoints. If the group subsequently proposes improvements to existing practices, it is less likely to be seen to be colluding with management to push for changes. The balance in the group will also need attention. It may be hard for one sceptic to find his or her voice amongst a number of enthusiasts.

In some situations, thinking through who can usefully form a group to achieve a particular purpose is less relevant. For example, in writing the specification for a new specialist computer system, composition may be determined by who has the necessary knowledge and experience. However, for all groups it will necessary to decide what is expected of its members and what will be their roles and responsibilities. Some questions to be answered are:

- who will chair meetings?
- will this and other leadership roles rotate?
- are group members there as individuals or to represent others?
- is it intended to cascade knowledge to other groups?
- will there be a facilitator?
- if yes, from outside or inside the organization?
- how big will the group be?
- who will decide these matters?

Group size is worth spending some time considering. As a rough measure generally if there are no more than six people, all will feel able to contribute. As the group gets larger some will feel able to say more than others. By the time it has as many as fifteen people, probably only a handful will confidently offer ideas and opinions and this is likely to decrease once there are over twenty.

> Regarding issues raised in 7.3, some of the lessons I have learned from involvement in the provision of customer care programmes in library and information services are:
>
> - participation of the most senior managers in workshops conveys a powerful message that the organization is serious about customer care
> - the presence of managers can inhibit some other participants
> - groups that comprise people fulfilling a range of roles in the service at different levels of responsibility can richly benefit from that breadth of experience
> - such a breadth of experience can result in some participants feeling it is not sufficiently tailored to their needs
> - a programme all department staff are required to attend can lead to resentment by those who feel they already provide adequate customer care
> - a customer care programme can challenge the attitudes of participants – it is more than passing on knowledge and does not readily lend itself to cascade training
> - an external facilitator can enhance a programme by providing such challenges to attitudes
> - some participants query whether a facilitator is needed – 'we could do this ourselves'.
>
> There is no consistent message from this learning. Each library or information service needs to consider its own requirements carefully.

The issues raised in this section are particularly pertinent when there is the scope to build a new group. Change often affords such an opportunity, whether for the short or long term. For example, a new structure in a university library and information service could lead to the development of new teams mirroring the arrangement of faculties within the university. The people within the new grouping may have worked in the organization for a number of years, but not as a team. For this group, expected to exist in the longer term, it will be necessary for members to clarify their roles and responsibilities, and establish how they are going to work together. In effect, though people may know each other, a new group has been brought into being.

7.4 The stages of development of groups

Effective teams are thought to develop and mature. Many writers on the subject refer to four successive stages, as set out below:

Stage one	*Stage two*	*Stage three*	*Stage four*
Forming	Storming	Norming	Performing[2]
Dependency	Counter-dependency	Cohesion	Interdependence[3]
Undeveloped team	Experimenting team	Consolidating team	Mature team[4]

When a set of individuals comes together as a group, they find it necessary to clarify its purpose. It is often a time when group members are uncertain and anxious, and feel a need to establish personal identity within the group. Subsequently groups often experience some conflict, frequently about leadership, authority and membership. There can be hostility between individuals, for example attempts to dominate discussions or ridicule others may be witnessed.

A group that has weathered these storms has the potential to establish group norms and practices. Examples are: how decisions will be taken, types of behaviour to be adopted, the degree of openness, trust and confidence that is appropriate. Individuals may test tentatively what level of commitment they can give to the group.

At all stages of development some level of performance will be achieved, though the performance of the immature group may be impeded by the agendas brought by individuals and by the process of developing. A mature group is likely to be most effective. Not all groups will arrive at maturity, and in terms of achieving its purpose, a group may not need to arrive at this stage.[5]

There is another stage not reflected in the diagram above, which is 'ending'. Changes in personnel, task and context can all bring about this outcome. Even though a group may almost be the same, one person leaving to take up a new job will effectively mean that the group needs to form again.

For a long-term group these stages can be spread over many months or even years depending on how much energy and time is used to address and make explicit the issues the group needs to address. On a one-day workshop a group will go through similar stages though will usually invest less energy, probably as group membership is temporary. The group may be 'performing' well before lunch.

In the context of change management it is important to recognize groups do, consciously or unconsciously, go through developmental processes that take time and energy. For some groups it may be important to provide resources to help them develop, for example in the case of a team building programme for the customer services section or the management of a newly converged service.

> There are many examples of interventions that can facilitate team development. As a team member or as a facilitator, I have found the following useful:
>
> - structured exercises that enable information about each group member to be voluntarily shared within the group building trust and commitment
> - the explicit agreement of 'ground rules' for how the group will work and behave, both during an awayday and in the workplace
> - examination of roles each person plays within the group – such as contributing ideas, being concerned to involve others in the group, ensuring the team sticks to the task in hand, obtaining information from outside the group
> - gaining knowledge of group processes, such as the stages of group development
> - psychometric tests giving insight into individual behaviour patterns
> - identifying and addressing the issues of concern to the group, which can vary from poor communication and low motivation to unclear aims and values
> - exercises intended to further develop interpersonal skills
> - tackling a task as a group and then processing what was learnt about how it was undertaken, including what each person contributed and what might have been different.

7.5 The developmental opportunities offered by groups

Increasingly the capacity to work effectively in teams is a requirement of staff employed in library and information services. Limited-life project groups, outside the line management structure, which bring together people to meet a specific purpose, are examples of such short-term groups that provide additional opportunities to learn more about team working. An organization moving towards a matrix structure from a strongly hierarchical structure may consciously try to involve everyone in a group contributing to the change, to introduce and model new ways of working.

An organization conveys powerful messages about its approach to management and change by the way it uses groups. Take as an example an organization whose objective is to empower staff by encouraging initiative and responsibility, and to move away from a centralized system that required permission for any service change. A working party is set up to plan and implement the refurbishment of a significant library site within a given budget. This group regularly updates the manager who has delegated this work. All appears to be proceeding well until a more senior manager visits the site and sees work in progress. Horrified by the new colour scheme, the senior manager insists that the whole scheme is reviewed by management, who subsequently require alterations. Management actions contradict rhetoric about empowerment. Members of the working party feel deflated, lose interest and this shows in the resulting refurbishment.

This chapter has explored:

- the uses to which organizations put groups
- the role of groups in change management
- matters to be considered when setting up groups
- stages in group development
- the staff development opportunities groups provide.

References

1. Handy, C., *Understanding organisations*, 4th edn, London, Penguin, 1993, 151.
2. Tuckman, B.W., 'Developmental sequence in small groups', *Psychological bulletin*, **63** (6), 1965, 384–99.
3. Bennis, W. and Shepard, H., 'A theory of group development', *Human relations*, **9**, 1956, 415–37.
4. Woodcock, M., *Team development manual*, 2nd edn, London, Gower, 1989.
5. Casey, D., 'When is a team not a team?', *Personnel management*, **17** (1), Jan. 1985, 26–9.

# Skills training

8.1 The need for skills training

Often skills training is seen as an early requirement in managing change: 'We had better set up a course on the new IT skills people require.' In reality the need is often recognized near the end of the change process, once staff have come to accept the new direction the organization is moving towards. At this stage there is frequently a demand for training from staff to enable them to take on new roles and responsibilities. When appropriate training is not provided, staff can be heard to make such comments as 'how can we be expected to take this on when we haven't been trained?'.

In Chapter 4 there was reference to equipping people to understand the processes of change, including management development. What is referred to in this section are the actual skills needed to undertake new tasks and roles.

8.2 Some examples of skills training

It would be possible to list in the context of change all skills that library and information services require of staff. Instead a few examples are given.

It may be the case that it is not only staff who need to be trained to facilitate the changes. Attention to the needs of users, board or council members and staff from other departments may also be required. For example, councillors may appreciate an introduction to a new service providing council information on the World Wide Web. An outcome of the enthusiasm generated may be to ensure ongoing support for the new service in terms of resources and good publicity.

The provision of such a new service might also necessitate staff updating their computer skills. The transition to a system using Windows may mean familiarization for all staff is necessary. For some the use of spreadsheets may be an imperative, while others will need to be able to develop web pages. With the rapid changes in technology, the list of associated skills required appears to be endless.

Another example of training requirements is the enhancement of skills following the restructuring of a service. Library assistants may be broadening their role to handle basic enquiries. These changes may require them to further develop the key interpersonal skills of paying attention, listening, questioning and responding in this context. In addition, they may need to familiarize themselves with the significant source materials they are likely to be using. The issue of when it is appropriate to pass on an enquiry can usefully be considered, so that it is understood that everyone in a library and information role is faced with that dilemma sooner or later – resolving the dilemma by referring the enquirer elsewhere need not be seen as a sign of failure. These and other elements of a training programme can lead to an enhancement of the service offered.

One of the culture changes happening in library and information services is the increasing awareness of the importance of the customer. For example, universities and colleges may have a vocal group of users paying their own fees who are prepared to demand satisfactory services. Staff development in this context might initially be used to foster a more responsive attitude to customer needs. Subsequently training may be required to help staff deal with difficult situations with users, be informed about their responsibilities towards people with disabilities, and establish guidelines about such matters as who should have priority when the service is busy, the user in person at the counter or a telephone enquirer.

8.3 Meeting training needs

There are many ways of meeting the types of training needs outlined above. These range from coaching and computer assisted learning to short courses and shadowing. An overview on this topic is provided in a companion library training guide on *Management of training and staff development*.[1]

Earlier chapters have referred to the topic of timeliness regarding introducing change. It is also pertinent to the meeting of training needs. Having embarked on the frequently difficult journey of change, staff who want to move on can feel disheartened and let down if the right training is not available at the right time. All the efforts to communicate and involve staff can be undermined.

This chapter has:

- noted the importance of meeting training needs relating to the acquisition of new skills
- provided examples of skills training resulting from organizational change
- indicated some of the methods of meeting training needs.

Reference

1 Whetherly, J., *Management of training and staff development*, London, Library Association Publishing, 1994.

 Working with resistance to change

9.1 What is resistance?

Resistance is always likely to show itself in responses to change. When planned changes are not implemented or occur in such a way as to be counter-productive, this could be an indication of resistance.[1] Statements such as the following might be heard:

- 'The ones who really need to go on a customer care course are the managers.'
- 'That new computer system will be out of date as soon as we get it – why not stick with the one that still works.'
- 'We tried organizing stock like that 20 years ago – it didn't help then and I can't see that it will now.'
- 'How can we deliver better services when we have less money?'

The likely outcome is an unwillingness, total or partial, to engage in the new behaviours likely to be needed for the change to occur.

9.2 Reasons for the resistance to change

Change is not automatically resisted by individuals. However, people will resist change if they regard it as harmful or likely to have negative outcomes. Each individual will have different reactions, assumptions and perceptions resulting in a range of emotional responses. Though these responses may be difficult for others to understand, for the individual those feelings exist. More widespread resistance may result from a shared concern, such as that arising from lack of knowledge or information.

Some of the reasons staff resist change are caused by:

- uncertainty resulting from:
  - lack of information
  - wrong information
  - fear of the unknown
  - loss of control
- the individual feeling:
  - afraid for her or his job/career
  - her or his status, power base and for existing skills are threatened
  - inconvenienced, for example, by change in location
  - bound by strong peer group norms
  - pressure to learn new skills
  - afraid of failure
  - reluctant to let go of the past/try out new ideas
- organizational culture:
  - that blames those who make mistakes

- that pays too much attention to custom
- that is weighted down by historical factors
- relationship:
  - where these are poor, or there is a need to make new relations
  - where there is low trust in the organization.

Sometimes people openly state their concerns, being conscious of the issues that worry them. At other times resistance is unconscious, perhaps because this change reminds the individual of past experiences: 'The workplace is a social organization and while the primary task is to effectively deliver an information service it also provides channels for individuals and groups to work through their own psychological agendas and to deal with their anxieties.'[2]

> I have become aware that my early experiences of the sudden loss of my father have had considerable implications for me when faced with change. For instance I have needed to know fully how the change will work so that I do not make mistakes or lose control of the situation. I now have some insight into how I have developed and can increasingly tolerate uncertainty and some imperfection in myself.

Resistance may be overt or covert, conscious or unconscious, and not always readily apparent. The insistence on careful analysis of what change is needed, followed by detailed planning, might be as good an example as any of trying to avoid or postpone change.

9.3 Working with resistance

Resistance is an aspect of change management that it is necessary to accept and to work with rather than try to overcome. A manager who bemoans the fact that staff still complain despite being sent on a change course is missing this point. An understanding of the change processes, some of which are described in this text, may help an individual. For example, appreciation that her or his responses mirror the transition curve and are not by any means abnormal may reassure that individual. However it will not in any way lighten anxieties about the need to learn computer skills, something that so far has been avoided, because without such new skills it will not be possible to do the job. Nor will it lessen fears that in the context of resource reduction posts may be lost.

There are approaches to change that aim to minimize resistance. An earlier chapter stressed the importance of communication. Sometimes managers feel that by holding back until the picture is clearer, especially when they have bad news to pass on, they are helping staff. In reality staff often sense something is being left out and trust in managers begins to falter. A situation can then arise when managers become frustrated that colleagues are too slow to accept the changes, forgetting that they have already had some time to come to terms with what the changes will mean for themselves.

Involving staff is also a way of working with resistance. If managers have all the changes mapped out with no opportunity for other input, it will not be surprising if staff have no sense of ownership. They will have been denied the opportunity to contribute in any meaningful way.

9.4 Training and development

Training and development have a significant role to play. The person worried about acquiring new computer skills is likely to be encouraged by receiving adequate, appropriate and timely training. If posts are being made redundant, workshops that help those leaving to look to the future can send out powerful messages to all staff that the organization is concerned about people and their lives. Similar support for managers involved in making redundancies might take the form of coaching, counselling or workshops.

Alison Crooks,[3] writing as State Librarian of New South Wales, suggests that staff development, though difficult to assess in terms of the concrete benefits it affords, 'constitutes one of the most effective means of getting new ideas and views aired in an organisation, and as such is an essential element in loosening up and getting change started'. In her organization they began with 'managerial and supervisory skills which included training in problem identification, analysis and solving, decision-making and action planning'. Later in her article she stresses that there needs to be a critical mass of staff who understand and are committed to the direction in which the organization is moving, who are also able and willing to take the necessary action that will make change happen. In such ways training and development can play a very significant part in equipping people with the necessary skills, knowledge, values and attitudes to bring about change rather than resist it.

9.5 The limitations of training and development

Though training and development have their uses, they also have limitations. Any conditions that inhibit learning will undermine their usefulness. For example, if staff cannot see the relevance of skills and knowledge that managers consider to be essential for the future of the service, they will not take such skills training seriously. Staff may feel it is an imposition, and resentment and resistance can be fuelled rather than diminished.

Training is not a substitute for good management. To take an example, a whole group of staff who work in the same department are sent on a customer care course. A hidden agenda by their manager is the hope that they will come back into the workplace transformed: no longer will they be people who are difficult and do not get on with each other. On the course they make up about half the total number of trainees. They do not know why they were sent on the course and start the day filled with resentment. Those present voluntarily gradually feel let down by the negative input from those obliged to be present. The trainer does his or her best to try to work with the difficult tensions present, but somehow any enthusiasm and energy initially found in the group diminish. The trainer, who had been led to believe that all trainees had chosen to come, is initially bemused and subsequently angry.

This example illustrates a situation for which training was not an appropriate response. Instead the manager might try to find out why the members of the group do not get on, and having challenged the situation in this way, arrange for a facilitated session to examine the issues stopping them from working well together. If the manager felt too close to the situation, it could be sensible to invite someone from another department or an external consultant to facilitate this session. It might also be pertinent to appraise whose judgement it is that they are difficult people, what this means and what behaviour changes might be needed by individuals in the group and possibly the manager.

A similar example, though perhaps more common, is when training is organized for a number of people in order to ensure that the one or two who really need it are covered. The others may often feel resentment and the people targeted for the training can miss it by going off sick or taking leave. Alternatively, well-managed appraisal invites a collaborative approach to identifying the individual and organizational training and development needs of each member of staff. A result is likely to be staff, encouraged by their managers, that are motivated to seek out appropriate training and development.

As suggested at the beginning of this chapter, there will always, for good reason, be some resistance to change. On occasions this will slow change down and indicate a need to re-engage staff by greater communciation and involvement. Sometimes there will be pockets of resistance resulting from an individual's need to slow down or stop the change. If the critical mass referred to above exists, in time some of those struggling to accept the change will probably decide it is time to go with the majority.

This chapter has:

- explored what resistance is and reasons for its occurrence
- examined why it is necessary to work with resistance
- noted the significant role played by training and development in achieving change
- identified some of the limitations of training and development.

References

1. Crook, A., 'Tough times and a large library: managing organisational change', *The Australian library journal*, Feb. 1990, 20-30.
2. Raddon, R. (ed.), *Information dynamics*, London, Gower, 1996, 91.
3. Crook, op. cit., 26.

10 Change agents

10.1 Who are they?

Everyone in the organization has the capacity to be a change agent. Though it is often perceived that change should be inspired and led by management, ideally an organization will be able to embrace the creativity and initiative of everyone. Otherwise energy and enthusiasm that might be made available are lost to the organization. That said, managers, including those responsible for staff training and development, and supervisors at all levels in the organization have a particular role to play. Staff look to those in leadership roles to provide models for themselves. For example, managers who require staff to go on customer care training but who are not seen to consider how they care for their own immediate customers, the staff, will undermine the message any training is intended to give.

10.2 Self-awareness

Probably the key to determining an individual's capacity to act as a catalyst for and implementer of change is the degree to which he or she embraces change. As hinted at in the above example, achieving change is not about requiring others to change while the manager stays the same. The change agent's knowledge and understanding of the following aspects of themselves will increase self-awareness:

- past responses to change, at work and outside
- mental maps of how change is planned and implemented
- beliefs about how change works
- past experience of change/how change was managed in the current organization
- skills possessed
- amount of control/choice felt by the individual at times of change
- the support available from within and without the organization.

Organizational change is complex because it is about achieving something different in the context of the range of experience, knowledge, understanding, motivation, needs and desires of the people who are stakeholders. Responses to change vary, because consciously or unconsciously people have choices. At the two extremes, they can resist by leaving the organization or can be so enthusiastic that critical analysis of the situation is put aside. Consequently the change agent, in addition to self-awareness, needs many and varied skills.

10.3 Skills for change agents

A simple model of the change management process, adapted from the work of Richard Beckhard and Reuben Harris,[1] is as follows:

- why change?
- what is needed in the future/happening now?
- how to get from now to the future
- how to manage during this transition.

The role of training and development will be to equip change agents to use appropriate skills throughout the process. Key skills are:

- strategic thinking and planning
- organizing ability
- communication
- interpersonal skills
- influencing and motivating
- negotiating skills
- handling conflict.

These are skills that to varying levels of performance are required of managers and supervisors. Most of them are needed by all staff working in library and information services. In the context of this text, which is focusing on the human aspects of change, some of these skill categories are further explored below.

10.3.1 Communication skills

The importance of communication was stressed in Chapter 5, which also outlined some qualities of effective communication. Explaining why change is needed and how the future might look are examples of significant tasks requiring well-developed skills. However, competence will not be sufficient. Situations involving change will also require signs that the communicator is enthusiastic, believes in what she or he says, and is committed to arriving at 'the future'. Others will quickly recognize false enthusiasm and lack of real commitment. Taking time to work out what needs to be communicated also allows opportunity for reflection and self-awareness by the change agents about their feeling towards the changes. This process of thinking through the change can lead to personal commitment.

10.3.2 Interpersonal skills

At all stages of the change process a high level of interpersonal skills is required. For example, a head of service might spend time *listening* to what staff and other stakeholders have to say about the inadequacies of the existing structure before developing a restructuring strategy. To encourage staff to offer their views, *questions* may need to be asked, and the questioner's understanding of responses confirmed by *summarizing* what has been heard. Such *active listening* helps facilitate the sense of involvement that most people need to have for change to proceed.

Some questions may be designed to *challenge*, without animosity, the current norms of the department. 'All enquiries have always come to professional staff at the information desk' might elicit the question: 'What would be the outcome if library assistants and their supervisors handled basic enquiries such as giving directions to stock?'. Such challenges can open up minds. They need to be a two-way process, for it could be the head of service that has limited insight into the potential for change. Likewise, *feedback* needs to be given and received.

Section 4.3 explored how to help people work through change. At this stage *empathy* can also play an important role. Besides the skills so far mentioned, having *patience* and the *ability to cope with other peoples' strong emotions* can be invaluable. In a difficult economic climate change sometimes results in losers, for example when posts are made redundant. The way in which people leaving the organization are treated is recognized to have an impact on those left in the department. Well-developed interpersonal skills will help staff handling such matters.

10.3.3 *Handling conflict*

Organizational change inevitably leads to some conflicts of needs, no matter how effectively communication has taken place or to what degree people feel involved. It is unlikely that everyone will be pleased by the changes. One person might relish the opportunity to learn new skills, another grieve for the loss of much used abilities no longer required by the department. In the latter case, the outcome will be resistance to the changes. However, if people feel their concerns are understood and appreciated, and if the reasons for decisions are satisfactorily explained, in time they will often embrace the changes.

10.4 Other qualities required by change agents

Key qualities of successful change agents also include *determination* and *resilience*. If change processes that have been started are given up, this can convey powerful negative messages that will hinder subsequent changes. The ability to live with *uncertainty* will be invaluable. If staff are to be truly involved, outcomes, though in the general direction intended, are likely to vary from the change agent's mental map of them. For some the whole process will be stressful, and their success at *managing themselves* will be crucial.

The achievement of change demands much of all involved. Mismanagement of the processes, so that working conditions become hostile, can lead to people being stressed to a degree that their health is damaged and they ultimately give up. Change can also provide a rich opportunity to learn new skills, increase self-awareness, observe how others handle particular situations, and analyse what has been successful and what could have been done differently.

This chapter has:

- noted the potential of everyone in an organization to be a change agent
- described key change-agent skills, in particular conflict handling and interpersonal skills
- identified other qualities usefully possessed by the change agent.

Reference

1 Beckhard, R. and Harris, R., *Organisational transitions: managing complex change*, 2nd edn, Wokingham, Addison-Wesley. 1987, 112.

 Creating the future

11.1 The learning organization

A thread running through this text is the notion that change is happening all the time and is something to be worked with rather than opposed. Presumably this has always been true, though today the rate of change seems closer to being on an express train than riding in a horse and trap.[1] This is challenging to most people and exciting to many.

Being able to change requires open minds capable of looking afresh at the world. Different or new pictures can emerge leading to fundamental shifts of understanding. Peter Senge[2] suggests that it is through such learning that 'we extend our capacity to create, to be part of the generative process of life'. He goes on to write that a learning organization is one 'that is continually expanding its capacity to create its future'.

In this context it does not seem unreasonable to suggest that an organization comprising people able to learn, to re-create themselves, is also an organization capable of continuous change.

11.2 Conclusion

A key concern of change agents is whether to focus on the 'task' or the 'people'. Imagine the outcome if attempts are made to introduce a new computer system that on paper looks superb, but which has not been discussed with those who will be responsible for its operation. At the other extreme the result could be an inadequate system if the task element were neglected. Though this text has concentrated on the human aspects of change management in the library and information world, in particular on training and development, it is recognized that our primary task is to provide services. Somehow both task and people need to be held in focus.

The notion of the learning organization appears to offer opportunity to the organization and the people it engages. Some large private-sector organizations have even set up their own 'universities' to encourage the development of learning, hoping that there will be spin-offs within the organization. Learning, open minds and change seem to go together. Individual needs are met because the opportunity to learn is regarded as a fundamental human need.

An outcome of becoming a learning organization, something more talked about than realized at present, is that we are all potential change agents. However, such a role is not without dilemmas, as Tony Page has shown in his book *Diary of a change agent*.[3] The role of change agent certainly requires an open mind, as Page puts it:

>Change is overdue and URGENT but . . .
>   if I rush I SLOW it down.

I want the change to be PREDICTABLE but . . .
> when I try to use Project Management methods they prove UNRELIABLE.

I want to discover ONE WAY of handling change that works reliably but . . .
> every change situation requires a DIFFERENT WAY.

The harder I PUSH for what I want the more others RESIST.

I want to PERSUADE others of why and how to change but . . .
> they only change when they DISCOVER why and how for themselves.

We need EVERYONE to come on board but . . .
> unless I allow CHOICE then people enlist grudgingly or compliantly.

I want OTHERS to change but . . .
> unless I change MYSELF they remain fixed.

References

1. Edwards, C., 'Change and uncertainty in academic libraries', *Ariadne*, 11, Sept. 1997, 6–7.
   Online at: http://www.ariadne.ac.uk/issue11/main/
2. Senge, P., *The fifth discipline: the art and practice of the learning organization*, London, Century, 1993, 14.
3. Page, T., *Diary of a change agent*, Aldershot, Gower, 1996, 189–90.

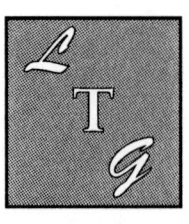

Select bibliography

Baker, S., Managing resistance to change', *Library trends*, **38** (1), 1989, 53–61.

Beckhard, R. and Harris, R., *Organizational transitions: managing complex change*, 2nd edn, Wokingham, Addison-Wesley, 1987.

Burnes, B., *Managing change: a strategic approach to organisational dynamics*, 2nd edn, London, Pitman, 1996.

Casey, D., *Managing learning in organizations*, Milton Keynes, Open University Press, 1993.

Corrall, S., 'Balancing the business', *Library manager*, **15**, Feb. 1996, 14.

Corrall, S., 'An evolving service: managing change', in *Networking and the future of libraries 2: managing the intellectual record: an international conference held at the University of Bath, 19–21 April 1995*, London, Library Association Publishing, 1995.

Corrall, S., 'The market for change', *Library manager*, **13**, Dec. 1995, 5.

Critchley, B., 'The myth of managing change', *Leadership and organisation development journal*, **17** (2), 1996, 48–52.

Crook, A., 'Tough times and a large library: managing organisational change', *The Australian library journal*, Feb. 1990, 20–30.

De Board, R., *The psychoanalysis of organizations: a psychoanalytic approach to behaviour in groups and organizations*, London, Tavistock, 1978.

Dutfield, M. and Eling, C., *The communicating manager: a guide to working effectively with people*, Shaftesbury, Element Books, 1990.

Fordyce, J. and Weil, R., *Managing with people: a manager's handbook of organization development methods*, Reading, Addison Wesley, 1971.

Grant, P., 'Supporting transitions: how managers can help themselves and others during times of change', *Organisations and people*, **3** (4), 1996, 38–40.

Handy, C., *Understanding organisations*, 4th edn, London, Penguin, 1993.

Harvey-Jones, J., *Making it happen: reflections on leadership*, London, Fontana, 1988.

Kanter, R. M., Stein, B. and Dick, T., *The challenge of organizational change: how companies experience it and leaders guide it*, New York, Free Press, 1992.

Managing change in the new public sector, edited by Roger Lovell, Harlow, Longman in association with the Civil Service College, 1994.

Morgan, G., *Images of organizations*, 2nd edn, Thousand Oaks, Sage, 1997.

O'Connor, C A., *The handbook for organizational change: strategy and skill for trainers and developers*, London, McGraw Hill, 1993.

Odini, C., 'The management of change in a library service', *Library review*, **39** (4), 1990, 8–20.

Page, T., *Diary of a change agent*, Aldershot, Gower, 1996.

Plant, R., *Managing change and making it stick*, London, Fontana, 1987.

Rogers, C., *Freedom to learn for the 80s*, Columbus, Ohio, Charles E. Merrill, 1983.

Sadler, P., *Managing change*, London, Kogan Page, 1995.

Senge, P., *The fifth discipline: the art and practice of the learning organization*, London, Century Business, 1993.

Spiegelman, B., 'Relationship management: helping employees succeed at change', *Library management quarterly*, **16** (4), 1993, 1, 5.

Stewart, J., *Managing change through training and development*, London, Kogan Page, 1991.

Stewart, J., 'Towards a model of HRD', *Training and development*, **10** (10), Oct. 1992, 26–9.

Stueart, R., 'Preparing libraries for change', *Library journal*, **109** (15), 1984, 1724–6.

Watzlawick, P. and others, *Change: principles of problem formation and problem resolution*, New York, Norton, 1974.

Wilson, D., *A strategy of change: concepts and controversies in the management of change*, London, Routledge, 1992.

Woodcock, M. and Francis, D., *Teambuilding strategy*, London, Gower, 1994.

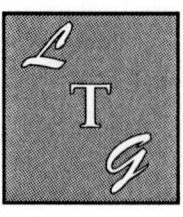

Examples
Sample working documents

1. Islington Library Service and Harriet Karsh:
   (a) *Managing Change Course for Islington Library Service Managers*
   (b) *Outline for Islington Libraries Managing Change Course*
   (c) *Change as a process*

2. University of Reading Library:
   (a) *Restructuring news*, 23 February 1996
   (b) *Staff preferences survey*
   (c) *Restructuring news (6)*, 16 July 1996

Please note these documents were provided by Sheila Corrall, University Librarian, University of Reading (formerly director of Library and Information Services at Aston University).

3. Leeds Library and Information Services:
   (a) *Staff survey*, September 1996
   (b) *Staff survey – key points*, December 1994 (n.b. first sheet of survey summary only)
   (c) *A library service to be proud of: meeting changing expectations – Aims and Programme*
   (d) *Meeting changing expectations – the way forward*, August 1996
   (e) Overheads from the *Meeting changing expectations* day.

The Leeds training programme was developed with Liz Howell: Liz Howell Associates, 21 Thorncroft, Englefield Green, Egham, Surrey TW20 0SB; tel. 01784 431242.

Acknowledgments
I wish to acknowledge and thank the individuals and organizations whose working documents are reproduced here.

Example 1a

KARSH
CONSULTANCY
HUMAN RESOURCE &
ORGANISATIONAL
DEVELOPMENT

Managing Change Course for Islington Library Service Managers

Aim:
To provide Islington Library staff with the understanding and skills needed to recognise and adapt to change and to apply their management abilities in a proactive as well as a reactive way.

Objectives:
Participants will have:
- Identified the factors that cause change to occur
- Recognised the changes that have occurred and are occurring in their environments
- Identified the culture changes needed to respond to a changed environment
- Clarified and practised the key skills needed to manage change

Programme

Day One	**Change and the Individual**
9.30am	Arrival and refreshments
	Sharing expectations
10.30	Sharing a model of change
	Unfreezing - Transition - Refreezing
12.30pm	Lunch
1.30	Driving and Restraining Forces for Change
	Resistance and Acceptance Influences
3.00	The Manager's Role
4.30	Close

Day Two	**Change and the Organisational Climate**
9.30am	Arrival and refreshments
	Organisational Culture and Climate
	The Change Culture
	Challenge and Support
11.30	Diagnostic Processes
12.30pm	Lunch
1.30	Reflecting on our own libraries and change
3.00	Action Strategies
4.30	Close

THE COACH HOUSE NIGHTINGALES LANE
CHALFONT ST GILES BUCKINGHAMSHIRE HP8 4SJ
TELEPHONE (+44) 01494 766100
FACSIMILE (+44) 01494 766604
DIRECTOR   HARRIET KARSH MA

1 HARLEY STREET LONDON W1N 1DA
TELEPHONE (+44) 0171 616 2208
FACSIMILE (+44) 0171 636 8789

VAT REG 589 6127 87
E MAIL 100705.1060@COMPUSERVE.COM

LIBRARY TRAINING GUIDES

Example 1b

KARSH
CONSULTANCY
HUMAN RESOURCE &
ORGANISATIONAL
DEVELOPMENT

Outline for Islington Libraries Managing Change Course

Day One--Change and the Individual
- Where does change come from ?
- Why do we implement change ?
- Why do we resist or accept change ?
- Change as process -- Unfreezing/ Transition/ Refreezing
- Consultancy groups to identify a change in our own situations that we want to implement focussing on:
    1. What do you need to do to get the change to occur or at least be tested? why? who? what? when? where? how?
    2. What is/are the role(s) you will have to play as a manager to get the changes to happen well?
- Effective communication model
- Roles that managers play
- Assessing the model

Day Two--Change and the Organisational Climate
- Factors that contribute to an appropriate climate for change
    -- Change - Challenge - Support
- Management Styles that help to foster positive change processes
- Factors that create an effective climate for change
- A model for implementing change
- The diagnostic stage
    -- the impact of change on the individual, the group of staff and the organisation's function and goals.
- Task to identify the questions one needs to ask to help:
    -- create an open climate where individuals (all involved including clients) can share their feelings and express how they perceive the change and its impact on them presently and in future
    -- the staff team, in light of individual responses, to re-examine the impact of the change on their collective functioning
    -- the organisation to address the implications of changes for their functions/goals bearing in mind the response to the outcomes of the consultation process with individuals and staff groups
- Planning for the imposed changes: for Individuals, Staff Teams, The Organisation

THE COACH HOUSE NIGHTINGALES LANE
CHALFONT ST GILES BUCKINGHAMSHIRE HP8 4SJ
TELEPHONE (+44) 01494 766100
FACSIMILE (+44) 01494 766604
DIRECTOR   HARRIET KARSH MA

1 HARLEY STREET LONDON W N 1DA
TELEPHONE (+44) 0171 636 2208
FACSIMILE (+44) 0171 636 8789

VAT REG 589 6127 87
E MAIL 100705.1060@COMPUSERVE.COM

EXAMPLES

Example 1c

CHANGE AS A PROCESS

KARSH
CONSULTANCY
HUMAN RESOURCE &
ORGANISATIONAL
DEVELOPMENT

Most theories of influence or change accept the premise that change will not take place unless the individual is motivated and ready to change. Schein (see below) suggests that it is therefore appropriate to consider and/or influence change as process which occurs over time and which includes three phases;

(1) **Unfreezing**
an alteration of the forces acting on the people or individuals such that their stable equilibrium is disturbed sufficiently to motivate them and to make them ready to change.

Accomplished by:-
- increasing the pressure to change
- reducing some of the threats or resistances to change

(2) **Changing**
the presentation of a direction of change and the actual process of learning new attitudes;

Accomplished by one of two mechanisms:-
- the person learns new attitudes by identifying with and emulating some other person who holds those attitudes

- the person learns new attitudes by being placed in a situation where new attitudes are demanded of her/him as a way of solving problems which confront her/him and which she/he cannot avoid. Although the person essentially discovers the new attitudes for her/himself, it is probable that these new attitudes will be essentially those which the influencing agent wishes to be adopted.

(3) **Refreezing**
the integration of the changed attitudes into the rest of the personality and/or into the ongoing significant emotional relationships.

Schein, in Davis and Scott, Human Relations and Organisational Behaviour, McGraw-Hill.

THE COACH HOUSE NIGHTINGALES LANE
CHALFONT ST GILES BUCKINGHAMSHIRE HP8 4SJ
TELEPHONE (+44) 01494 766100
FACSIMILE (+44) 01494 766604
DIRECTOR HARRIET KARSH MA

1 HARLEY STREET LONDON W1N 1DA
TELEPHONE (+44) 0171 636 2208
FACSIMILE (+44) 0171 636 8789

VAT REG 589 6127 87
E-MAIL 100705.1060@COMPUSERVE.COM

LIBRARY TRAINING GUIDES

Example 2a

RESTRUCTURING NEWS

A message from the Librarian to all Library staff

As it is more than a month since I circulated my paper on the Future of the Library and it will be a few weeks before our planned open discussion meetings can take place, I am writing to everyone to provide an update on how things stand and also to put right some misunderstandings.

I am very grateful to the staff who have given up their time to the "Sounding Board" group, who are acting as change advisers to the Senior Management Team. After only one meeting, they gave us lots of useful suggestions and they have also been very helpful in picking up questions and concerns which are understandably worrying people. The open meetings which we are arranging will give you all the chance to raise these points and others, both individually and in groups; but as I don't want people to worry unnecessarily, I am dealing with the queries I know about at present.

Timing of changes

I am proposing to implement the new staffing structure this summer (1996) because I think change is urgently needed and the long vacation is a good time to tackle this sort of major project. The same principle applies to putting in a new computer system, which we plan to do the following year, in summer 1997. In fact, this is the first realistic opportunity available to us as it would have been difficult to complete the European Union tendering process in time for this year, even if we had started last October. But in both cases - the new structure and the new system - detailed work must begin as soon as possible, as there is a lot of planning to be done.

The new structure

The staffing structure I have proposed has been designed specifically for Reading University Library and is significantly different to the structure implemented at Aston. There is an obvious similarity in the choice of Faculty Teams as the main 'organisational unit', but that focus reflects a general trend in both libraries and other service organisations to restructure in ways that enable better liaison with their main customer groups. At a recent SCONUL seminar on "Structures for the future" which Julia and I attended, there were 57 higher education institutions represented and the faculty team approach emerged as the favoured model for university libraries of the future.

There are important differences between the Reading and Aston structures in the composition of the senior management teams, and in the prominence given to Collection Management. At Aston, traditional technical services ceased to exist as separate specialist units, largely because the library had moved so significantly away from the acquisition of printed materials toward electronic information provision, and it had also been reduced in size. At Reading, in contrast, I think we need to pay a lot more attention to the planning and management of our Collections, and I expect a university with a strong humanities and social sciences orientation to continue to be heavily dependent on printed publications. This is why I have brought David Knott into the Senior Management Team as Head of Collections, and I have proposed having a group of specialist individuals and teams to be responsible for different aspects of managing our collections, which will include important issues such as weeding, storage and retention policies. In addition, I have proposed a senior management post at Reading with an overall responsibility for human, physical and financial resources, and I also envisage 'middle management' roles for these areas, because I think a library of Reading's size and type needs more co-ordination and support at the centre than was necessary at Aston (where most of this work was handed over to Faculty Team Managers).

The areas where I think some of the things I did at Aston are applicable to Reading are more to do with management 'style'; for example, improving communication with staff at all levels, and involving them more in decisions - including the details of planned changes!

The new system

As already indicated, we plan to replace our existing library housekeeping system during summer 1997. I expect the new system to do all the things our present one does (but better) and a lot more besides. In particular, we need to have online facilities for book ordering and periodicals check-in.

Example 2a continued

It would also be good to have a wider range of self-service options for users (for example, self-issue, renewals and reservations) as this ought to help reduce queues at the issue desk. The formal tendering process is similar to a staff recruitment exercise. We have to advertise our intention to purchase a new system, then send further details of our operational needs to interested suppliers, who can then apply to do the job. We then have to draw up a short-list, invite those people along to tell us what they can offer, and finally make a decision on the basis of which system we judge will best meet our needs at reasonable cost. The process is actually a bit more complicated than that - inevitably - it will require quite a lot of hard work by those involved.

We are planning to form a Project Team for this, and its membership will include staff from the operational areas affected (eg cataloguing, circulation, reference services) as well as those with particular technical expertise or special interest. This team will be responsible for seeing the whole process of specification, selection and installation through to conclusion, but I expect to involve others in various parts of the exercise. For example, in a similar exercise at Aston, the project manager invited all library staff, computer services staff, students and selected academics to help test and evaluate the short-listed systems - with the incentive of free cups of coffee! To give people a clearer idea of what is involved, I have asked John Matthews, who managed the project at Aston, to spend a day with us explaining the process. This meeting will take place on Friday 8 March in our 1st floor seminar room, and will be open to both the core project team and others interested to come along for all or some of the sessions (but subject to the usual constraints of space and time).

Consultation process

We have now set dates for the open discussion meetings during the first two weeks of the Easter vacation. We wanted to hold these earlier, before the end of term, but unfortunately had problems with availability of both rooms and people - including difficulties with my own diary, as I have several external commitments that I agreed to undertake before accepting this job. The meetings will take place at 9.30 and 2.30 on Friday 29 March and Tuesday 2 April (two meetings each day, all in the Finzi Room). In addition we have planned a fifth meeting for 9.30 on Wednesday 8 May for those who cannot attend in the vacation. On the assumption that most people will want to come along, and also to help managers of frontline services, we shall timetable everyone for a particular session, but staff can swop with each other - or opt out altogether - if they wish. We are still working out the exact format for the meetings, but they will include an introductory presentation from me, followed by plenty of opportunity for questions, comments and discussion.

By the time of the meetings, we expect that the senior management team will have agreed after discussion with individuals concerned who will take on most of the larger areas of responsibility (ie the Team Manager roles specified in my paper). The allocation of other people to teams will happen later, as we shall need to have more detailed discussions about the numbers and grades of staff required for each area. There will be some opportunity for people to express interest in moving on from their current specialisms to something different, but we shall have to balance any individual preferences against the Library's need to retain sufficient expertise in essential operations. The final decisions on "who goes where" will rest with the senior management team, but we shall consult others (eg section heads, supervisors, etc) on the things we ought to take into account and our actual proposals for putting people in teams. The open meetings will provide the chance for everyone to raise queries and make suggestions about this process.

The whole restructuring process will need a lot of careful planning over the next few months, and I hope many staff will become involved in this more detailed work. We already have the Sounding Board/Change Advisers group, who are helping senior management by acting as a channel of communication and suggesting to us how best to manage change and consultation. I expect to form several other groups to work out in more detail how best to organise day-to-day operations and services in the new structure. Although our timetable has slipped a bit from that outlined in my paper, we may still consider holding one or more facilitated workshops off-campus to move things forward. Even if you are not personally involved in a project or working group, you will have the opportunity to put forward your views. I welcome comments and questions from everyone - as individuals or groups; in person, by phone, in writing or by e-mail - and you can either contact me direct, or send them via managers, section heads or "sounding board" members.

Sheila Corrall   23 February 1996

LIBRARY TRAINING GUIDES

Example 2b

READING UNIVERSITY LIBRARY   STAFF PREFERENCES SURVEY

After Easter, the Senior Management Team will begin the task of putting people in teams. We are keen to take account of individuals' interests and experience as far as possible, but feel that we don't have enough information at present, especially about colleagues' previous experience. We shall also be talking to managers/supervisors, section and floor heads, etc, before taking any decisons.
If you have any difficulties in answering this questionnaire, please ask for help.

Please note that we expect to have tasks at many levels in most areas of work, either on a short-term or continuing basis. The new structure will enable us to involve more people in different activities, on both an ad hoc and permanent basis, so we are inviting everybody to express their interests and preferences. We also hope that it will enable more people to try new things more often.

Name   Grade

Current post (Library Assistant / SLA, etc)

Section / Floor / Branch

Full-time / part-time / term-time
If part-time, please state hours per week

1   Do you want to carry on and develop your current technical, reference or other specialism?

    Yes / No

2   Which academic department or departments are you interested in supporting?   *Please see attached list*

3   Do you have any knowledge or experience of particular relevance to the departments indicated above, or to any others - eg from a previous job, personal interest, family background, etc?

4   Do you have language skills - at any level - that might be put to good use in the new structure (eg shelving, bib-checking, cataloguing)?

    All offers welcome, from rusty school French to degree level!
    Please state language(s) and provide some comment on your proficiency.

Example 2b *continued*

5   Are you interested in spending part of your time working in / on any of the following areas?   *Please circle*

   Archives, Manuscripts & Rare Books   Buildings & Space

   Library Finance   Personnel & Training   Library Systems

6   Are there any skills you are keen to acquire, practice or develop further?

7   Are there any Process Teams of special interest to you?   *Please circle*

   eg   Book Orders   Cataloguing   Periodicals

   Issue / Enquiry Desk   Short Loans   Interlibrary Loans

8   Are you interested in taking on a co-ordinating role for any special responsibilities which might benefit from a Library-wide view in the interests of standards and consistency?   *Please circle - or suggest other areas*

   eg   Induction   Information skills / user education

   Part-time students   Overseas students   Other users with special needs

   Public relations / publicity   Quality assessment   User surveys

9   Are you interested in being considered for a supervisory or leadership role, now or in the future - either on a short-term project or in a continuing team?

   Yes / No

10 Please add any other comments you wish to make about our future plans or your place in the new structure.

Please return this questionnaire to Sheila Corrall by Thursday 4 April
(or as soon as possible)

Example 2c

RESTRUCTURING NEWS (6)

A message from the Librarian to all Library staff

It is seven weeks since I last circulated a general news update. We had some comments and queries on restructuring issues at the meetings in the Staff Room following the Curators meeting, but not everyone attended those discussions, and as I am about to go on leave for three weeks this seems a good time to send out another round-up on recent developments and current concerns.

What's been happening in the meantime?

As well as the informal open meetings in the Staff Room on 26 June and 1 July, I have led two discussions with line managers to consider their roles and responsibilities in the new structure (on 17-18 June) and with the assistance of Bryan Cowan, Director of the Centre for Academic Staff Training and Development, I have held two workshops (on 1 and 8 July) to consider the current operation and future direction of the Bindery. This work is now being taken forward by a project team led by Geoff Gardner. Also during this period, we interviewed and appointed staff to fill the remaining management positions in the new structure. In addition - though not directly related to restructuring - I have had a series of meetings with Deans and Sub-Deans (involving the Deputy Librarian and the relevant Faculty Team Manager) which I have used to update them on how far we have got with forming Faculty Teams and to point out that development of 'tailored' services will be a gradual, evolutionary process. The Deans have all stated their support and enthusiasm for our development plans.

Line management arrangements

At the meetings with managers in June I presented a list of things that I think are part of the management role (which are summarised on the attached sheet). I also cleared up some misunderstandings about reporting arrangements, in particular who will 'line manage' Library Assistants in the Faculty Teams and how soon the new reporting structure will take effect. Eventually, when people are spending most of their time on Faculty work, Liaison Librarians will report to Faculty Team Managers (or Team Leaders, in the case of FLSS) and Library Assistants will report to designated Liaison Librarians - who will then become their line managers. However, as we have often acknowledged, it will be some time before we reach that situation. An important principle of line management is that the person to whom someone reports is the one best placed to observe and guide their work; if staff are supervised by two or more people, then their line manager should be the person who supervises them for most of the time. So as long as staff spend more time on Process work than Faculty work, they will continue to be line managed in the Process Team. The new line management structure will not therefore take full effect until our work has shifted in that direction.

Culture and style

At the bottom of the sheet produced for line managers, I added a few points on the way I want us to work together. These comments reflect the sort of management style and organisation 'culture' (= the way we do things) which I feel will help us to operate most effectively as a team. COMMUNICATION is a vital part of this, and it is probably the single most important responsibility of management to ensure that people are properly informed. However, communication is a two-way process, which means that everyone has to play his or her part responsibly and actively - if people don't listen, or if they don't express their views and concerns it is rather hard for me and others to respond to them. DECISION-MAKING is another area where I am keen to see changes so that there is less of a 'top-down' approach and more involvement of people at the operational level in decisions related to day-to-day work. The final point on the sheet simply acknowledges that even in the best-run organisations MISTAKES happen - at every level - and the sensible response is not to blame someone, but to find out what went wrong and why, and try to prevent similar errors in the future. Mistakes are very often the result of poor communication! There are lots of other topics that could be discussed under this heading - and no doubt will be in due course - but if there are any particular issues you feel need to be addressed sooner rather than later, please tell me, your manager, David Read or any member of the Change Advisers Group.

Different team approaches

Another query at the line management workshops was about the acceptability of teams adopting different management arrangements. To some extent this is inevitable, given their differences in size and membership, so we might expect less specialisation and more 'multi-tasking' in the smaller teams than in the larger ones. But there are other good reasons why different practices may be appropriate - such as the spread of skills among team members, the service needs and priorities of the faculty served, and any physical constraints on day-to-day operations. The important thing will be for each team to reach a shared understanding of how it will operate so that people know what is expected. Flexibility and responsiveness will be the keys to success here.

Clerical 3 posts

I am sorry that we have not yet advertised the promised Grade 3 Supervisory Library Assistant jobs. There have been several other personnel matters requiring urgent attention (including front-line service vacancies) which have taken priority over the last month. Although we are now running into the difficulty of getting people together over the holiday period, I hope that the necessary discussion and documentation will be completed shortly, and we can then move forward as planned. The thinking behind these posts is that we plan to reduce substantially the involvement of professionally-qualified staff in Process team operations when we implement the new computer system, and we therefore want to appoint suitably-experienced staff to take on some of the supervisory and administrative work which does not require a professional qualification. If these appointments can take effect from next term - rather than waiting until the new system is installed - it will mean that the people concerned will have the chance to move into their new roles gradually and also be fully involved in choosing and introducing the new system.

More general matters

ANNUAL LEAVE. Some people have asked whether there will be more restrictions on annual leave during termtime as a result of restructuring. It is difficult to give a definite answer, but I don't see any particular reason why this should be the case. The same principles for leave-taking will apply as at present, namely we shall try to be even-handed in dealing with people's requests for leave at particular times, but we must ensure that we have sufficient staff to maintain essential services. Eventually the new structure should result in a larger number of people trained in a wider range of tasks, and this should give us more flexibility - but how soon we reach this position will depend on how much time we can find for training and development alongside day-to-day activities.
CLEANING. One of the items of concern at the last meeting of the Change Advisory Group was the cleanliness of the public service areas of the groundfloor. This is a common problem in libraries, as the busy areas tend to get dirty more quickly and there are fewer opportunities to clean them thoroughly. No obvious solutions have come to mind, but those concerned are investigating.
FIRST AID. Another query raised by the Change Advisers was about the small number of trained First Aiders among our staff. We discussed this recently at the Senior Management Meeting and noted that the University's training provision was limited. We agreed that it was especially important to ensure that senior staff undertaking minimal service duties were adequately prepared in this respect and we decided to ask our qualified First Aiders to front some video presentations for colleagues, probably during lunchtimes or some other convenient slots over the vacation.

Next steps

There will be more changes and developments over the rest of the summer. Work on upgrading the 3M security system and changing the entrance and exit gates in the Main Library is almost complete, and this will be followed by the removal of the cloakroom and locker fittings to create a more attractive reception/refreshment area. Many people are already busily working on group or individual projects, and one of the things David Read will be doing as part of his new role is to create a register of project work so that everyone can be kept informed of what's going on. In September (as you may have picked up from the Library List) I shall be inviting people to help me review our mission and objectives, and set out priorities for the next session.

Sheila Corrall   16 July 1996

LIBRARY TRAINING GUIDES

Example 3a

SAMPLE

STAFF SURVEY **SEPTEMBER 1996**

The aim of this annual survey is to discover **your** views of the library services in Leeds and enables you to comment on how things are going. Please complete and return to Grace Kempster by **Wednesday 16 October** In 94, I got 160 responses, in 95, I received 93. It is really up to you to have your say - directly and in confidence.

1   What do you enjoy *most* about working for Leeds Libraries? — *Working with the Public*

2   What do you enjoy *least* about it? — *Not enough stock*

   *H*ave any of the aspects you enjoy *least* changed during the last year? *No.*

3   How would you rate communications, i.e. knowing what is going on - and being able to pass on your views and opinions [please circle]

   Poor   Excellent
   1   2   ③   4   5
   Please give reasons/suggestions:

4   How would you rate the library services you offer? [Please circle]

   Poor   Excellent
   1   2   ③   4   5
   Please give reasons:

> **Example 3a** *continued*

5 What do you think about the **direction** i.e customer focus, information role, income generation etc. of the library service?

Strongly disagree with it   Strongly agree with it ✓

1   2   3   4   5

Please comment:

6 Do you think the service is changing?

For the worse   Not changing   For the better

1   2   3   4   5

Please comment:

7 Please give up to *three* areas in which you would like to see the service developed in the year ahead:

More non fiction Adult Books
Books to help children's homework

8 Please list here any other comments or suggestions [continue on another page if necessary]

If you would like to talk further on any of the points you have made in this survey, please indicate   YES/NO

Optional   NAME   LIBRARY/SECTION

LIBRARY TRAINING GUIDES

Example 3b

STAFF SURVEY -KEY POINTS   December 1994

This is a summary of key points i.e. those made by several people. If you would like a full version - please ring Anne Ford on 0532 478330/1.

WHAT ARE OUR STRENGTHS?

Replies

94	Over a third of the total replies stated that **the staff** are our greatest asset: flexible, expert, caring for users, responsive, committed to the service with an attitude to overcome difficulties in a positive way and an ability to cope with limited resources.
14	staff also noted the relationship with and the loyalty of **our users** as strength
3	noted that in-house training is a strength
29	note stock as a strength, though many go on to qualify this - due to reduced book funds, we are to some extent living on our inheritance
22	note the strength of collections in Central, again with similar qualifications as above
8	note the reserves system as a strength, needing to be more widely promoted
24	note it is good we are a free service
18	note that the branch libraries are serving the needs of their communities being friendly places
4	note the value of meeting rooms
10	particularly note the network of libraries as a strength as regards access
11	note computerisation and the changes it will bring is a strength in the future

Example 3c

LEEDS LIBRARY AND INFORMATION
SERVICES

A library service to be proud of
MEETING CHANGING EXPECTATIONS

AIMS

- To create a common understanding of the meaning and significance of being customer focused in a time of change.

- To recognize the importance of every individual's role in contributing to service excellence.

- To further develop skills in delivering consistently good service, particularly in difficult situations or when under pressure.

- Through action plans, to consider ways in which ideas and learning points from the course can be carried over and applied by library staff in their own libraries.

Example 3c *continued*

LEEDS LIBRARY AND INFORMATION SERVICES

A Library Service to be Proud of
MEETING CHANGING EXPECTATIONS

Programme

8.45   Arrival and coffee

9.00   **INTRODUCTIONS**

- Aim and Overview of the day

THE MEANING OF CUSTOMER FOCUS

- Who are your customers? (External and internal)
- What is service excellence?
- What is the significance today for libraries?
- A changing world and rising expectations

10.30   Coffee

COMMUNICATING A PROFESSIONAL IMAGE

- 'Moments of Truth'
- Ways we communicate - face to face and on the telephone

REALLY LISTENING

- Building rapport
- Gaining and clarifying understanding
- Empathic and Reflective Listening

12.45 - 1.30   LUNCH

Example 3c *continued*

Leeds Library and Information Services
Meeting Changing Expectations

The Programme Contd\.....

p.m. **MAINTAINING A POSITIVE APPROACH**

- Attitudes and their consequences
- Aggressive/Submissive/Assertive behaviours
- Managing ourselves under pressure

3.00 Tea

HANDLING DIFFICULT SITUATIONS

- The importance of feedback (internal + external)
- Handling complaints effectively - the 8 A's formula
- Enforcing regulations
- Managing awkward customers

MOVING FORWARD

- Review and summary
- Personal Action Plan
- Course Evaluation

5.15 CLOSE

Example 3d

IMPORTANT   TO EVERY MEMBER OF STAFF

August 1996

MEETING CHANGING EXPECTATIONS   -   THE WAY FORWARD

I hope you got a lot from the day with Liz Howells or Jan Jewars, as I did.
This was not just another training day - it blew the training budget and cost £38 plus relief for everyone to go - why?

Because focussing on the customer is vital for our survival and future.
We won't have one unless we constantly improve and develop this. That's what the re-structuring is all about - to make us all closer to the front-line.

When I am arguing for more resources, the questions are - why? Have you got more people using the library and information service? Are the people of Leeds seriously bothered if the library has an increased book fund or not?

Every one of us has to work hard to ensure that **each person** has a satisfying and memorable experience **every time** they use the service. If they don't and we're just OK in our customer service, we're dead.

You may say, well we haven't got the resources - not enough staff, books or poor buildings My answer is - how do we get them then? Just asking will not cut any ice with decision makers. We have to work hard to get noticed and valued by our users - then they'll be storming their local Councillors' surgeries demanding that their library service is better funded.

This course is just the beginning.

During the next two months you will be visited by a **Policy Forum ROADSHOW** - we want to talk with you about the importance of the course as the start not the end of our journey towards excellent customer service.

See you soon

Grace

EXAMPLES

Example 3e

CUSTOMER SERVICE STRATEGIES FOR LIBRARIES

Towards the millennium:
Improving customer service in libraries

Leeds Library & Information Services

- ever changing to meet growing expectations
- may not realise staff expectations for growth or more resources
- a tough message to sell

Leeds Library & Information Services

- every difference counts in the competitive arena
- customers will NOT allow second chances

Leeds Library & Information Services

Strategy in Leeds - 1

- re-think the dispersal of staff
- handling the reference interview
- CCT - Customer Contact Time
- a visible presence
- finding out how people REALLY feel
- refreshers to customers
- spread the word

Leeds Library & Information Services

Strategy in Leeds - 2

- First impressions - a new awareness
- customer service standards
- choice at the shelves
- Meeting changing expectations
- "We must manage the difficult and stressful situations - that's when customer service really counts"
- "Any service organisation has to effect real and constant cultural change to thrive in the future"

Leeds Library & Information Services

And onwards

- change champions
- customer service standards
- money for suggestions
- "constant reminders until it becomes a way of life are required - it will take years of continuous effort"

Leeds Library & Information Services

LIBRARY TRAINING GUIDES

Example 3e *continued*

Stakeholders - and choice

- Do what you uniquely do best - or die. The choice is yours
- Where shall we compete?
- Making a stand - for a service
- Who are the important users?
- Decide now

The customer view

- unfriendly, boring and dated
- friendly and helpful
- imaginative, dynamic, enthusiastic and memorable
- expect to be delighted

Who wins?

- imaginative service recovery solutions
- the most imaginative frontline staff
- working smart, hard and finding your competitive edge
- support and discipline in an uneasy mix
- get complex messages across

The future - full circle?

- The customer is always ... relevant
- signs of people power everywhere
- hopes for partnership
- energetic advocacy
- strong sense of ownership
- convince them - they can make a difference

- Continuous evolution of customer service strategies just a little ahead of our customers may be the only investment worth making in these uncertain times
- It should still be - customers

Index

action learning 17
attitudes to changes 8

behaviour change 12, 13
behaviourism 3
bereavement 14, 15

change agents 1, 35, 38
change management theory 3
closed systems 5
commitment 10, 22
communication 10, 18–21, 22, 32
complexity of change management 7, 35
continuous change 22, 38
critical mass for change 33

development and training
 benefits 33
 definition 12
 exercises 4, 15, 16, 27
 facing up to change 16
 interventions 13, 27
 limitations 5, 33
 meeting training needs 30
 methods 16
 non-staff training 29
 timeliness 30

emergent change 7
emotions 16, 37

fundamental change 1, 7

Gestalt psychology 3, 4
group dynamics 7
group dynamics school 4
group process 4
groups
 compostion 25
 duration of 24
 norms 5
 purpose 24
 size 25
 stages of development 4, 26
 types 24

implementing change 10

improvement 1, 7
individual
 experiences of change 9
 responses to change 9, 14, 35
individual perspective school 3
informal communication networks 20
involving staff 10, 22–23, 32

leadership 21, 23
learning
 opportunities for 12, 28
learning organization 1, 38
Lewin, Kurt 7
loss 14

magnitude of change 9
management development 17
managing change 1
minimizing resistance 32

need for change 9
norms of behaviour see under groups and organization norms

open systems 5, 6
organization norms 5
organizational change 1, 7

personal development 1
planned change 7
proactive change 10
problem solving group 17
process see under group process

reactive change 10
resistance 22, 31–4

self-awareness 35
skills
 change agent 35
 communication 36
 computer skills 29
 customer care 30
 handling basic enquiries 29
 handling conflict 37
 interpersonal 36
stakeholders of change 18, 20, 35
strategies for change, choice of 9

team development 27
teams *see* groups
timing 9, 20
training and development
  see under development and training
transition curve 15, 16

triggers of change 8
turbulent change 8

verbal communication 18

written communication 18